Reau Campbell

Around the Corner to Cuba

Reau Campbell

Around the Corner to Cuba

ISBN/EAN: 9783337193874

Printed in Europe, USA, Canada, Australia, Japan

Cover: Foto ©Andreas Hilbeck / pixelio.de

More available books at **www.hansebooks.com**

ON THE CARNIVAL DAY.

TO

CUBA

BY REAU CAMPBELL

AUTHOR OF "WINTER CITIES IN A SUMMER LAND;" "RAMBLES FOR SUMMER DAYS;" "54;"
"THE CORNER OF THE CONTINENT;" "VI AND JACK;" " HOOK AND I;"
"CUBA IN EASY LESSONS;" "PALM LEAVES OF FLORIDA, A TRIP
FROM PASSADUMKEAG TO OKEECHOBEE;" ETC., ETC.

1889:
C. G. CRAWFORD,
NEW YORK.

NEW YORK :
PRESS OF C. G. CRAWFORD,
49 & 51 PARK PLACE

AROUND THE CORNER TO CUBA.

HE little Island around the corner of the continent is a land of pure delight, where every day is summer, where the whistling blizzards from the northland simmer to the gentle fanning of a zephyr as on a May day, where summer clothes do business in December, where fans are a legal tender all the year round and overcoats always at a discount; where blue mountains lift up in craggy peaks to the lighter blue of the brightest skies, where rolling hills topped with feathered palms and cocoas roll down to valleys luxuriant, green with waving fields of cane, or the long leaves of that weed which so fragrantly ends in smoke and delightful reveries; where pretty women are clad in the lightest and laciest of costumes, nor sigh for seal skins; where age and beauty go hand in hand, and every man grows anarchistic when he thinks about it, to overturn the laws that make señorita and duenna go in double harness; where there is more play than work to keep Jack from being a dull boy, where the advertiser must do as he advertises, or hang; where soft sensuous melodies delight at the opera or the dance, and the vivacious notes of animated music excite at the bull fight; where the spelling-book maker who wrote, "I had some green corn on a plate in July," did not live.

That's Cuba.

To many, Cuba has been only the scene of a romantic novel, the memory of a geography lesson, or the whence-ness of good cigars, and to travelers a far-off country that few ever got to, but always remembered with *mucho gusto* and was the subject of many a fascinating reminiscence told to the listeners at home, held entranced by such tales of travel; but to-day Cuba lies at our very doors.

Another reminiscence of Cuba, not attended by a superabundance of fascination, was the long voyages in wintry seas, necessary to reach the shores of that queen of the isles of summer. The memories of Hatteras were not always pleasant to recall, and the traversing of the Gulf, not at all times plain sailing. In mortal dread of the inevitable *mal de mer*, many a winter tourist has applied the only remedy for that ill by staying ashore, preferring the little ounce of prevention rather than be compelled to try the pounds of alleged cures, and perhaps, threw up a trip that was to be the realization of a tour through an enchanted land, whose beauties were known only from the tales told by more venturesome travelers.

The memories of my journey to and through Cuba are all pleasant ones. It was the leaving behind of snow-clad hills, and the whirling wheels of a Pullman whitening the car with the flakes scattered from its pathway, soon rolled me under brighter skies, through the orange groves of Florida, down where the palm trees grow.

On a long pier, out over the water, the wheels stopped, and I passed from my berth to the cosiest stateroom, which was to be my home during my short "life on the ocean wave."

Leaving from Port Tampa, where the change from the cars to the ship is without transfer of distance, and may be likened only to a change of cars across the platform, the voyage is like that over a lake of placid waters, down the coast of Florida to Key West, where a stop is always made for the discharging and receiving of freight. There is time at Key West for a ramble or a drive around the island ; for just how long, ask the captain.

This is only a ferry from America to Spain. The ship leaves Key West, and while you sleep crosses the Gulf Stream, and when you wake the sun may be shining over the towers of Morro Castle, and your awakening be in a newer world to you, but an older one than your grandfather's.

MORRO CASTLE.

Ships sail from New York and New Orleans, sailing down the east coast of the United States or across the Gulf of Mexico, as of old, and those who like a long sea voyage may have their choice of those routes to Cuba. But if the "ferry" is preferable, take the Pullman to Port Tampa and cross over as I did.

THE GETTING READY.

When a journey to foreign ports is to be made, a passport must be thought of. But when the destination is Cuba, that state paper is wholly unnecessary. So says the Queen Regent of Spain in a royal decree promulgated July 30, 1887, and the only protective document needed is the certificate of a notary public that the bearer is an American citizen, and he may have the freedom of the island, to go where he listeth, and depart on the homeward journey when he will, with no one to question or require *vised* papers.

MONEY

is a passport most anywhere, and a most valuable and convenient one everywhere, and in Cuba, as other places, is essential, though not more so than elsewhere, the hotel and traveling expenses not being above the average tariff.

It is not necessary to buy Spanish gold or Cuban paper before starting, because the bankers on the Island will pay the highest prices for greenbacks, American gold, or New York exchange, and the tourist may suit his pleasure or convenience as to what shape his funds are in, and, after arrival at destination, can deposit his home money in an American banker's vaults, and draw the Cuban currency or Spanish gold, as it is needed for daily use. A letter of credit from reliable bankers in the United States will also be honored by American bankers in Cuba.

Hotel bills and railway fares are payable in Spanish gold, or its equivalent in Cuban paper ; purchases in stores or shops are charged in gold or paper, the information being announced with the price. Cab fares, tickets to theatres and places of amusement are priced in paper; also cigars and liquid refreshments have a paper value.

The paper currency is very much depreciated; one American dollar will usually buy two and a half in Cuban paper—our dollars and cents translate to *pesos y centavos* in Cuban; in Spanish gold (oro español) an *onza* is worth $17.00; half *onza*, $8.50; a *centen*, $5.30; a *doblon*, $4.25; an *escudo*, $2.12, of American money.

Postage to the United States is five cents (*cinco centavos*) per two ounces or fraction of an ounce. Cablegrams to New York, fifty cents per word, with a corresponding tariff to other cities.

The tourist will find it to his interest to call on an American banker soon after arrival, and post himself financially as to rates of exchange, etc. The bankers will be found to be most courteous and obliging, and ready to assist their compatriots at all times.

THE ARRIVAL AT HAVANA.

A ship not sailing under the Spanish flag, cannot enter the port of Havana between sunset and sunrise, a custom long enforced by the government, which, if it was intended for the tourists' pleasure, could not have suited him better, because the ships' schedules are so arranged that arrival is made at sunrise, and when she sails up under the guns of Morro Castle, with the brightening daylight tinging the eastern sky and showing the frowning walls of Morro and Cabaña, and behind them the distant hills through whose crowning palm trees the earliest sunshine is streaming, the picture is wonderfully beautiful, and a look to the starboard shows the city just awakening, and ready to give you the warmest welcome.

At the entrance of harbor on the east side is Morro Castle, just back of which on the same side is Cabaña Castle. On the other side, opposite Morro, is La Punta, the forts constituting the defense of the city from attacks by sea. Sailing past these forts the ship comes to anchor in mid-stream. No foreign vessel ever goes to a pier at Havana.

The "doctor's boat" comes alongside just after the ship has entered the harbor, and by the time anchorage is made opposite the

ARRIVAL AT HAVANA.

Custom House, the health and port officers have examined the papers and given permission for the passengers to disembark.

In the meantime there have come out to meet the ship what seems to be a hundred country wagons, afloat with their wheels under the water—these are the boats that are to take the passengers ashore—boats with bowed awnings, for all the world like a country wagon down in Tennessee; these are propelled by oars or sail (I mean the boats not the Tennessee wagons) and the fare to the Custom House is 25 cents. There have come out, also to meet the tourists, agents of the various hotels, agents polite and attentive without being obtrusive, speaking English and Spanish, and unless one is posted or speaks the language, it is well to select the hotel and turn your baggage over to him, as some of the hotels have their own boats and carts for transfer of baggage. The rowing to shore is but the work of a few moments, and the novel ride winds up at the stone steps of the

CUSTOM HOUSE.

Here all baggage must be examined by the Customs officers, who are most liberal and courteous gentlemen—you declare your baggage, that there is nothing but your personal effects and no dutiable articles, a hasty look to carry out the law, the thing is done and you may proceed to your hotel—there are no delays except when there is a crowd of tourists, then, if desired, keys may be left with the hotel agents and the travelers go on to

THE HOTELS.

The tourist, especially he who has listened to the yarns of the old-time travelers, will be most agreeably surprised when he discovers the many excellencies that pervade the best hotels in Cuba, in parlor, dining-room and bed-chamber. All of the old objectionable customs and arrangements have been done away with, and very many innovations introduced that brings them very near the modern standard of the American hotel.

There is a register, of course, and you are expected to write more of your personal history than usually appears on the register of your native land. The book is ruled in columns, and each has its heading; the first is *Fecha de Entrada*, date of arrival; the next is *Nombres*, names, then the *Naturalidad* or nationality; next *Residencia*, residence; then the one that ladies, at least, should not be required to fill out, the one which shows *Edad*, age of the guest; the next is also peculiar, it is *Estado*, the state of the arrival, married or single, I suppose, as the average is sober. Then follows the *Profesion* column, to show your profession; after that is the one showing *Procedencia*, whence you went, then *Fecha de Salida* tells date of departure, and the last column is *Numero de Orden*, giving the number of guests.

These columns are not now imperatively used, but in the days of wars, revolutions and insurrections, when they wanted to know all about everybody they were required to be filled out, but the war taxes remain as at home, and a revenue stamp must be placed on the register opposite each name.

Bell-boys are plenty and very properly do not wait in the office but on the floor where they attend, so when you ring he does not have to tramp up four flights to find out what is wanted, tramp down and then back to your room. The Cuban bell-boy waits near the annunciator on each floor, ring your bell and he is at your door in a moment, and *not* with a pitcher of ice-water—they don't drink ice-water in Cuba —at least Cubans don't; an earthen jar, very porous, so that the water does not get too warm, is placed in each room and kept filled with fresh water, so that only Americans call for ice-water, and that is brought in a glass, as it is not supposed that anybody wants much ice-water.

Fountain de la India

An early morning ring from the average room means coffee, in Spanish *café*, but from the American occupied room it may mean "cocktail," for which there is no Spanish word, and the American one is adopted and understood, and I may say, well made.

The bell-boy is usually very bright and can do odd jobs in translation for you, in a small way. If you hand him the water-jug and don't know how to tell him what to put in it, he will fill it, bring it back and say *agua* (ah-wah) with a look of pity on your want of education, though he is willing to teach you, as he evidences when you write a note to the office for pen and ink, he brings it back and hands it in with the remark "*la pluma y tinta*," so you'll know next time, if your memory serves you, and the bell-boy may not know you have paper and envelopes, and if he brings them it is with the further information that they are called "*el papel y sobres*."

The Cuban bell-boy is a complete success.

The bedrooms of the Cuban hotel are novel in the extreme. The floors are tiled with a brownish red tiling, with rugs in front of the bed, dresser, table and toilet stands. The bedsteads are of iron, brass or mahogany, all with the whitest of canopies, of light material, furnished with snowy sheets and pillows; and, as an agent of one hotel told me on my first arrival in 1886, if I would go to his house, I would find mattresses on the beds. It was easy for me to imagine that a mattress would be an immense advantage to a bed, and hard for me to understand how any bed could do a successful business without one. But I learned later that in summer days there is too much warmth in a mattress, and that sleep was only obtainable on a stretch of canvas corded to the bedstead, or on a woven-wire mattress and a sheet, and that in the early days of tourist travel this style of bed was used the year round. The covers used are light and scarcely ever needed in winter.

Coffee is served at any hour desired, in your room or in the dining-room; breakfast from nine till noon; dinner from five to eight P. M.; and in the dining-room is where the most grateful surprises await the tourist. The *menu* is ample, and the dishes nicely prepared. There are many familiar ones and some mysterious, but I was never disappointed in one, and soon was not afraid or suspicious. The vegetables and fruit were fresh and crisp—no hot-house forcings or stale importations, but just in from the gardens. The fish were superb, being taken direct from the water to the frying-pan, it being against the law to sell a dead fish. They must be taken alive and kept in floating coops till sold. The meats were sweet and well prepared, the poultry young and tender. This was my experience wherever I stopped. Ice is an expensive luxury in Cuba, and all productions must be consumed at once, nothing can be kept in the market. Eggs must be new-laid always, or no sale. Milkmen don't drive wagons, and can only water their stock in the way provided by nature—give it to the cows to drink—and when he sells milk, he drives his herd around town and milks at the door of his customer, and the out-put is immediately boiled.

The rates at Cuban hotels are about the same as at the same class houses in America, and are conducted on both plans, American and European; but it is best to understand the terms when you register—which is a good rule in this country as well. The figures are from $3 to $5 per day, wines extra. The price includes room, coffee and fruit in the morning, breakfast and dinner. Families and parties can have suites with private parlors and dining-rooms. English-speaking chambermaids are in attendance on the ladies' apartments, and all toilet arrangements are complete on each floor.

Every hotel has its corps of interpreters, who are courteous and obliging and will attend parties to the theatres and on sight-seeing tours. These gentlemen are on the hotel staff; but it is customary to remunerate their service—it must be left to the guest's appreciation of the service to say what the amount will be—but I will say that in most cases the money is well earned.

Now that the tourist is comfortably bestowed in one of the good hotels of Havana he must see the city—nobody walks, it must be done

IN A CAB.

There are thousands of them, easily found night or day in any part of city. Each cab is a four-wheeled victoria, equipped with one horse and one driver and generally speaking all in good condition, capable of making good time, and at a rate that is astonishingly low—the fare to any point east of Belascoain avenue is only 40 cents, in paper, for one or two persons, equal to 16 cents in United States money; for three persons the fare is 50 cents; beyond the avenue the fare increases to 50 and 60 cents.

If there are several places to visit the cab had best be secured by the hour at $1.35 for two or $1.85 for three persons per hour—if so engaged say *"por hora"* when you get in and tell the driver where to go.

How?

Oh, you don't speak the language. Just call the name of the place, it is not necessary to fatigue yourself by translating the phrase "drive to," the driver will understand the situation, if you get in and say *"Correo"* he will "drive to" the post office, or *La Punta*, the point opposite Morro at the terminus of the "*Prado*," the *Catedral*, *La Merced*, *San Augustin* if you are going to church; or "*Plaza de Toros*" if your taste carries you to the bull fights the cab will—or if to the theatres say "*Tacon*," *Irijoa* (ery-ho-a) or *Albisu*. To the railways, "*Ferro-carril de la Bahia*," "*Ferro-carril de la Habana*," or "*Ferro-carril del Oeste*." If to any particular street call the name of it and look out for the number of the desired address. If you get muddled beyond the hope of extrication and your vocabulary is exhausted call the name of your hotel, go back, get the interpreter to speak for you and start out again.

The best way to call a cab in Havana is to whistle for it (if you can), and when you have attracted the driver's attention, motion with your hand for him to go away and he will drive right up, (this reminds me they do many things upside-down in Cuba, the key holes in the doors are made that way).

In driving through the streets it is easy to become confused, but if you will remember that the streets are so narrow that a city ordinance requires to drive down certain streets and up others—so if your driver does not go down the one desired, don't be alarmed, he will go down the one next to it and come up the other.

At the end of trip, or the time the cab was taken for, pay the driver, or he will wait at the door and count time on you; an imported trick from the United States.

These cabs of the Victoria pattern are an innovation in Havana, on account of the narrow streets were introduced some time ago to supplant the unwieldy, long-shafted and hard-to-turn-round *volanta*—an easy-riding vehicle, propelled by one horse in shafts and another buckled alongside to carry the driver, or, rather, postillion, as he rides the other horse—but both horses travel so far ahead of the volanta that very few of them could get into any one part of town at a time, and in case of a block, must have gone to the country to turn round. The increase of business down town drove the volanta from Havana—but they might be used to great profit and pleasure in the parks and drives, and it is a wonder some enterprising liveryman does not re-introduce them. Every American would take a ride in a volanta just to talk about it at home. Volantas are used now only at Matanzas, for excursions to the Yumuri Valley and the Caves of Bella Mar.

Besides cabs and volantas, there are other and cheaper methods of locomotion in Cuban cities. I refer to the inevitable and irrepressible.

HORSE CARS AND STAGES.

The fares are ten, twenty and thirty cents in paper, according to the distance traveled. One line at Havana leads out Charles III. avenue to the Botanical Gardens, Base Ball Grounds, and the *Plaza de Toros* (Bull-Ring), another to Cerro, one along the shore in front of the city, another to the famous Henry Clay Cigar Factory. Cars start from Plaza San Juan de Dios every fifteen minutes from 6 A. M. to 10.30 P. M.

CENTRAL PARK BY GASLIGHT.

The stages have a uniform fare of twenty cents in paper, which is higher in proportion than the cabs, being about eight cents in American money. Starting from Plaza de Armas and the Castillo del Principe, they run to Jesus del Monte and the Cemetery.

There are no "bob-tail" cars, you are not to be trusted to "put the exact fare in the box." A uniformed conductor punches in the presence of the passenger.

There is another way to see the city which involves still less outlay of capital—that means of going which was in fashion in the days of Adam. The

WALKS ABOUT HAVANA

are attractive, but they must not be long walks, and are most pleasant in the evening. Walking in Havana is not popular at best, the sidewalks are not built that way, many of them are scarcely three feet wide and some in the business district are less than two, while in the new city there are some that will compare favorably with other cities. It is said that the curbs in the old portion were originally laid to prevent wheels from defacing the walls of the buildings.

In the Campo de Marte, on the Prado, in Central Park, are excellent promenades. On certain evenings of the week fashionable Havanese drive to Central Park, stop opposite the Statue of Isabella, and listen to the music of the military band, and promenade up and down the plaza. Here you may see la Cubana in all her dark-eyed beauty, with snowy laces and mantillas falling gracefully over head and shoulders. The carriage stops at the curb, in an instant it is surrounded with cavaliers, dark and black mustached. La Señorita enjoys the homage so gallantly paid ; the duenna, I think, often pays strict attention to the music, to give the girl a chance, but if she left the carriage, the duenna went also, perhaps with watchful eye and ear only half turned to the music. The Central Park is one of the places to walk to in the evening when the band plays, but if you want to sit and rest, chairs are twenty cents each. Another walk in the morning, is along the Prado from the Statue of India to La Punta, all the way under the laurels that shade the street.

From any of the hotels one may also walk to

THE THEATRES.

Havana has elegant places of amusement that would ornament a greater city. The Tacon is the third largest theatre in the world, La Scala at Milan and the theatre at Seville, in Spain, only being larger. The Tacon is the home of opera in Havana. There are five tiers of boxes, one above the other, extending all around the house. These boxes seat six people, and are patronized by the *élite*—always in full dress. Behind the boxes is a wide passage-way, through which one may pass from one box to another, or serves as a promenade between the acts—and between the acts is filled with promenaders, with visitors, and with lookers-on through the Venetian blinds into the boxes occupied by some especially brilliant party—and it is said that boastful belles brag on the size of the crowd that assembled behind the box and watched the beauties within.

The Albisu is the theatre of the Casino—the swell club of the city. Every Cuban city has its Casino Club, noted for its balls and entertainments.

The Irijoa (e-ry-hoa) is called the summer theatre because it is arranged with Venetian blinds from the roof to the foundation, instead of solid walls, and by a simple turning of the slats admits the breezes that nearly always blow in Cuba ; this theatre is surrounded by a garden into which the audience empties itself to drink *penales*, eat ices, or smoke between the acts, and are recalled to the auditorium by a bell like unto that on a locomotive.

Managers of Cuban theatres are particular as to music, it must be good ; the orchestras may be mixed as to race of the performers, but their performances are satisfactory ; often in third class theatres one hears as good or better music than in the best American theatres.

Each performance at a place of amusement has its president appointed by the
municipal government, his duties are to settle differences between the audience and
the performers and to preserve order. A Cuban audience is critical, insists on the
granting of encores when demanded, and goes behind the scenes between the acts ;
this is their prerogative. It is told of a prestidigitateur who advertised the decapita-
tion act, but whose wires and paraphernalia were so disarranged by his visitors behind
the scenes that he could not illusively cut off his own head, and was disposed to cut
that part of the programme as he could not carry it out actually without physical
discomfort to himself ; the audience insisted ; the president decided for the audience ; the illusionist was in despair, but did not lose his head ; he went to work,
repaired his traps, and did the trick amid the applause of his audience.

At every theatre or other place of amusement a box decorated with the coat of
arms and colors of Spain is reserved for the Captain-General and remains vacant unless he attends or sends a representative. Seats are also reserved for the press, and
names of the papers are pasted on the seats.

The prices of admission are about the same as American theatres, the price at the
Tacon is $5 and $6 in paper, at other performances $3 to $4 is the figure—some theatres sell a seat for a single act for a dollar—and at most theatres the general entrance
is only $1 to $1.50 but does not include a seat. Seat coupons are collected by the
ushers prior to the opening of the last act. Speculators sell almost the entire house
on the sidewalk, though reserved seats may be bought beforehand. It is best not
to pay a speculator the first price asked, as he always tacks it on and will reduce
before he will miss a sale.

After the opera is over the audience vacates the theatre with a rush, and coming
out, unanimously holds a handkerchief over the mouth and nostrils to prevent the
breathing the night air, some get into carriages and are whirled home but many
gentlemen and ladies frequent the cafés and enjoy ices, coffee, and other refreshments.

The gala days for theatres and other amusements are Sundays and church feast
days, then are they all filled to overflowing, to standing room only, as are the

COCK AND BULL FIGHTS.

These take place on Sundays only, and both are popular sports in Cuba. The
cock fights are of minor importance compared to the other. They take place in a
pit very much like the wheat and stock pits in a Chicago or New York exchange,
and the calls of the bettors are about as intelligible in one as the other. Around a
ring about twelve feet in diameter are arranged seats like unto a circus—here sit the
lookers-on. The owners of the birds and the bettors are everywhere, in the ring
and out of it, on the seats and under them. On a balance suspended from the roof
are hung bags, each containing a chicken—they must balance exactly—which is the
only fair part of the fight. They are taken out of the bags, and with long keen
knives fastened to their spurs they are placed in front of each other—it is not a question of courage or endurance, but as to which gets the first strike—one fowl is
always killed and often both, and it takes only a minute to settle the difficulty—the
dead cock is removed and two fresh birds introduced with the same result all day
long. At the

PLAZA DE TOROS,

or Bull Ring, the programme is pretty much the same, only on a larger scale.
Bull fighting is to Cuba and Spain what base ball is to the United States, and the
" bloods " of that country become amateurs in that sport as they do at ball in this—
and also as in this country the stars are imported and the company, also the bulls.

In the season of 1886-7 Mazzantini came from Spain with his *banderilleros* and *picadores* and brought eighty thorough-bred bulls. Bulls are   in Spain for their fighting qualities as race-horses are in Kentucky for their speed, and the great *Matador* was paid $40,000 for thirteen performances.

Mazzantini received a classical education at Rome, and after graduation returned to Madrid and was rapidly promoted in the railroad business. He was an amateur *matador*, and was so proficient that he soon became a professional and quickly became a star.

To THE BULL FIGHT

The attraction in 1887-8 at Havana was Guerra, called *Guerrita* on account of his small stature, but a *matador* of the first magnitude ; his debut is of but recent date, and, like Mazzantini, was a star at the conclusion of his first performance.   On that occasion the *primer espada* was killed by the first bull, his assistant disabled, Guerrita was left alone to kill his eight bulls of the performance, and he came out of the ring famous.

Guerra also brought his own company and imported his live stock ; his terms also. thirteen times for $40,000.

The "Plaza de Toros" is in shape very much like the cyclorama buildings of

America, only much larger; inside is a monster amphitheatre seating thousands of people. Encircling the arena is a high fence or barrier with a foot-rail about eighteen inches from the ground, on the inside, on which the performers step and leap over the fence when too closely pursued by the bull, landing in an open space between the audience and the ring.

The opening of the performance is brilliant and exciting, the audiences are nearly always large, sometimes numbering fifteen to twenty thousand, all eager for the fray. Gay colors are everywhere, bands are playing the liveliest airs, and all is excitement. The feeling of an American under the circumstances is one of amazement and anxious expectation. There is a grand flourish of trumpets, a gaily caparisoned horseman dashes in, gallops to the President's box, a key is thrown to him, it is the key of the door leading to the pens where the animals are kept; the horseman catches the key, woe be to him if he don't, and gallops back to the entrance and disappears; if the key is not caught the man is hissed out of the ring. Another flourish of trumpets and loud huzzas from twenty thousand throats announces the coming of the company.

It is, indeed, a brilliant spectacle, the *matadores* and *banderilleros* on foot and *picadores* on horseback, all clad in the gayest, gaudiest costumes, in all colors and gold

THE COMING OF THE COMPANY.

embroideries, they march to the President's box: the President is a municipal or State officer, and has full direction of the proceedings. He is saluted by the company and the fight is ready to commence.

Now the wildest excitement prevails, and the scene is a perfect picture of pandemonium; all eyes are turned toward the low strong doors under the band stand; they are thrown open, and from a darkened pen the bull bounds into the ring. As he passes under the rail a steel barb, with ribbons attached, showing the breeder's colors, is fastened in his shoulder. He gallops to the middle of the ring, stops and looks about with fear and astonishment. He is a grand-looking beast. Surprise and fear give way to rage, he paws the earth and snorts in his frenzy, and discovering the red cloak of the *espada* starts towards him on the run. The man goes over the fence, but not too quickly, for he has hardly disappeared before the bull's horns are thrust through the boards. The animal turns and spies a horse, and woe be unto the horse, his day has come; the *picador* with his lance is totally unable to keep the bull from goring the horse, and it is killed on the spot. The horses are not valuable ones, being old veterans retired from service, feasted and fattened to friskyness for this occasion, are blindfolded and ridden in to certain death. Another man is chased out of the ring and another horse

THE FALL OF THE PICADOR.

severely wounded; a signal from the President and a bugle call directs the horses to be removed.

Now comes the really interesting feature of the performance, the thrusting of the *banderillas*. The bull is alone with his tormentors, it is a contest between skill and brute strength. A banderilla is a wire about two feet and a half long, on the end is a very sharp barbed point, the wire is covered its entire length with colored paper ribbons. The banderillero is the man who places them in the bull's shoulders, he must stand in front of the animal, without flag or cloak, must stand still and wait the attack. The bull, maddened at his audacity, starts at him at full speed, the man steps out of his way gracefully, and skillfully thrusts the banderillas in the bull's shoulders as he passes by (they never speak as they pass by), as soon as the

BANDERILLERO CALLING THE BULL.

animal can check his headlong speed he turns, now furious with rage, he turns, only to find another banderillero with two more banderillas. These and two more are thrust into his shoulders, all hanging there. Bellowing now, he is wild.

Another signal from the President instructs that the bull has had enough and must be killed—this is where the *matador*, the *primer espada*, distinguishes himself, his skillful killing of the bull by a single thrust of the sword is what determines the brilliancy of the star. The matador must face the bull, sword in hand, and await the attack, it is assassination to strike while he is at rest and calls for hisses and missiles from audience. The blood-red cloth or *muleta* is flaunted in front of the

THE THRUSTING OF BANDERILLAS.

bull. The maddened animal closes his eyes and makes one more dash for life and falls in death, the sword of the *matador* is thrust between the shoulders to the hilt and has pierced the animal's heart.

Wild bursts of applause fill the air, hats, canes, cigars by the bushel are thrown into the ring by the delighted spectators, men shout and sing, ladies wave their handkerchiefs and mantillas, the matador bows his acknowledgments, throws the hats and canes back to their owners, who seem grateful that he should honor them thus.

The band plays, the gates are opened, three gaudily decorated mules harnessed

INCITING THE BULL WITH THE MULETA.

abreast are driven in, a rope is thrown over the dead bull's horns and he is dragged out.

The wait between the acts is not more than a minute, the bugle calls, the low doors open and another bull gallops in, and thus till six are killed at each performance. The skill and agility of the performers is something wonderful and consists in holding the red cloak in such a way that the bull rushes for the cloth instead of him who holds it, the bull shuts his eyes and does not see the man as he quickly steps to one side and escapes, but often he must save his life by flight and a leap over the barrier around the ring, and I have seen an infuriated bull follow him right over into the circle between the ring and seats.

THE THRUST OF THE SWORD.

When the last bull is dead the audience disperses in good humor, if the fights have been well done, if not, they hoot and hiss, throw chairs and other missiles into the ring and it would seem they would mob the fighters, it is either that or to unhitch the horses and drag the carriages to the hotel.

The tickets for the bull fights are sold at high or low prices, according to the magnitude of the star performing at the time, ranging from six to eight dollars for seats on the shady side, and three to four on the sunny side of the amphitheatre; private boxes are sold at twenty and thirty dollars, besides the cost of general entrance, two to three dollars for each person, thus it is that bull fighting is an expensive luxury, it comes high but they must have it—the American goes once anyhow, and if it were not for the horse feature would go oftener, but it is not likely that part of the play would be cut to suit so small a minority of the patrons.

THE CARRYING AWAY OF THE BULL.

Speaking of cigars as thrown to the bull-fighters in approval of their daring—I have wondered if the cigar-thrower doesn't often think "you have fought the bulls and came out safe, now try that cigar"—for they were wicked looking cigars.

About the first thing an American thinks of on landing is

WHERE TO GET A CIGAR?

and nine times out of ten his first smoke in Cuba rivals in bitterness the first of his life. A good cigar to the Cuban would seem vile to the smoker from the United States, and those on sale at the stands are not intended for other than Cubans. Ninety-nine per cent. of Cubans smoke, but none chew tobacco—I mean ninety-nine per cent. of the men. Cigarettes are charged to the ladies, but the act of smoking never came under my observation—though they do not object to smoke—the men smoke everywhere and at all times and under all circumstances.

Cigars are made for all nations, and a different cigar for each nation—hence do not buy a cigar till you know where to get one made for this country, or you will lose faith in the reputation of Cuba's chief product. Different nations require different sizes as well as qualities—Europeans using the largest and Americans the smallest cigars. The eight-hundred-dollar-gold-wrapped *Soberanos* of the Henry Clay factory is twice the size of any American cigar, and would cost $1.50 each—not much sale here—these go to the nobility of England, while the dainty little *Bouquets* or *Perfectos* come to America. There are stands where you can buy cigars you will like, and for

half the money they cost at home ; but it is best to go to the factory and buy a sup-
ply for two or three days' smoking—any of the factories will sell a single box, and
the proprietors will be found to be most courteous gentlemen ; and when one finds
what elegant cigars can be sold for very much less than
home prices one becomes a free trader at once, no
matter how much of a protectionist before.
The laws of the United States do not allow
the traveler to bring a single cigar
past the Custom
House ; if the officer
passes a few dozens it is
purest courtesy—the fallacy of
"49" or "99" being admitted free
of duty has no foundation in the statute
—and when an American smokes a cigar in
Cuba it is with a peculiar satisfaction at the thought
that he is beating the government out of the duty,
and I believe all smokers are free traders after one trip
to Havana, and to make a returned tourist vote against the tariff
it will be only necessary to puff the fragrant blue smoke in his nostrils.

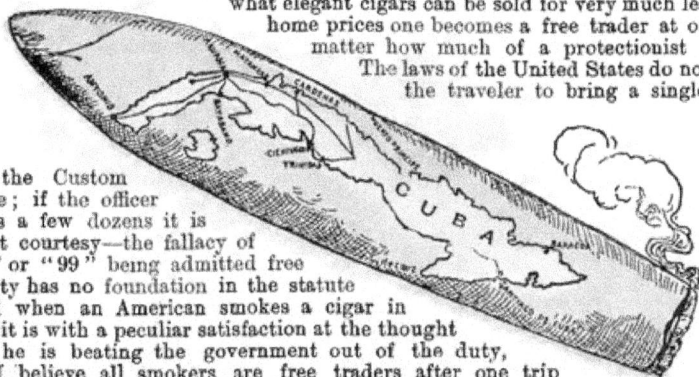

All smokers in Cuba do not smoke cigars, and the pipe is seldom ever seen ; very
many indulge in

CIGARETTES.

But they are not the rank, dudish thing of America. The Cuban cigarette is made
of the same fragrant tobacco that has made the island famous the world over.
Cigarettes are made by hand and by machinery, with paper wrappers and tobacco.
One factory has a single machine that turns out a hundred thousand cigarettes every
day—"La Honradez," of Havana—and the output is nearly half a million every day.
I can't describe the wonderful machine, the invention of a Virginian. The tobacco
is thrown in a hopper, passes out through a tube on to a ribbon of paper, a mile or
two long, like the paper of a telegraph ticker ; the paper with the coil of tobacco resting on it, passes into another tube and is curled up and pasted around the tobacco,
is cut off at proper lengths and drops into a basket "just as easy." It all seemed simple
enough, as I saw two small boys stand by, shovel in the tobacco, turn on the bands
and make the wheels go round.

In riding about the city,

THE CHURCHES

must not be forgotten. The Cathedral is the principal one but not the oldest. San
Augustin was formerly a monastery, and was built in 1608, and the Nunnery of
Santa Clara in 1644, while the Cathedral was not commenced till 1656 and completed
in 1724. One of the numerous tombs of Columbus is in the Cathedral ; here the
ashes of the great discoverer lie beneath a bust of himself, the tablet bearing an
inscription in Spanish, which, being translated, means

> O ! Remains and image of the great Columbus,
> A Thousand Ages endure preserved in this Urn,
> And in the remembrance of our nation.

The fashionable church of Havana is "La Merced," built in 1746, is attended by

CATHEDRAL AT HAVANA.

the elite of the city, and is a place of special interest to tourists; the decorations are superb and there are some fine paintings.

High Mass may be heard at the Cathedral and any of the churches on Sundays and feast days at from 8 to 9 A.M., but they are always open and visitors cordially welcome.

The others are Santa Catalina on O'Reilly street, where repose the bodies of the martyrs Celestino and Lucida, brought from Rome as relics.

The Nunnery of Santa Clara and the Monastery of Belen are places of interest.

There are no pews or seats in Cuban churches. The people kneel on the floors while the prayers are said, there being no long, tedious sermons to listen to. Some worshippers bring a small cushion to kneel on or a small camp-stool.

It is permitted to visit the different forts and fortifications—the principal one is

MORRO CASTLE,

and the next Cabaña. Visitors are admitted only by permit from the military authorities, which is easily obtained through the hotel agents, or the American Consul can put you in the way to get the necessary papers. Drive to the Muelle de Caballeria and take a boat (at a cost of 25 cents each) to the east side of the bay, less than a mile, present your papers to the very civil military gentleman in charge, who will courteously send a soldier with you, and you will be glad you came. The bay you have just crossed is smooth and calm as a mill-pond, but just at the base of the castle's north walls the sea is as wild as the mid-Atlantic. The tower of Morro Castle is a light-house, showing a flash-light of exceeding brilliancy fifteen leagues to seaward. The view from the ramparts is a magnificent one,—to the west the city of Havana lies spread out, to the southeast the palm-covered hills extend away to the mountains, to the north the boundless ocean lies, the waves washing in and out, way out to where they meet the skies. Morro Castle is connected with the other forts on the same hill by a tunnel under ground.

All the forts and castles may be visited and there is no word of particular advice to give except to bear the necessary papers, and while in the forts avoid making notes, as the act might be misconstrued.

There is one thing that must not be forgotten ; a visit to the

MARKETS.

They are all attractive ; the best time to go is early morning. The Tacon is the leading market, and there is none finer anywhere, the Colon has been recently completed, and the Cristina is the oldest. Step into a cab and drive to either, dismiss the cab, for an hour or so may be most pleasantly spent ; there is everything for sale in the Havana markets, fish, flesh and fowl, dry goods, hats, boots and shoes ; chickens are cut up and sold in pieces ; if a whole one is not wanted, you can buy a drumstick or a wing—anything from a piano to a banana ; there are fresh vegetables in December as we see them in New York in July, and every variety of tropical fruit at surprisingly low prices, and there are some fruits that many Americans never heard of. There is a special market for fish, which should by all means be visited ; the fish are kept in coops, so to call them, sunk in the bay, and it is a good market regulation that no dealer is allowed to sell a dead fish, he (the fish) must be "alive and kicking" when the sale is made ; ice is too high for use in the fish market. By all means, include the markets in your tour of the city, so you can tell at home of seeing green peas, beans, green corn and lettuce in the open market in January; that you saw wagon loads of pine-apples offered at five cents apiece, and oranges, with the leaves yet green on the stems, for a cent. The markets are good places to get cheap souvenirs to take home with you.

In driving about the city, one will not be impressed with the exterior of the

CUBAN RESIDENCES.

There are several palaces in Havana, belonging to Spanish noblemen, which, if you are fortunate enough to obtain the entree, will prove a most interesting feature of your visit. The average Cuban residence does not make much display on its exterior, and many are not particular as to who their neighbors are, or where the location. The line is drawn between their homes and the world by the street wall, and whatever may be outside that wall, has nothing to do with the inside ; outside may be a dirty, squalid street ; a peep through an archway will show a court, white and clean, with marble floors and stairs, playing fountains, growing plants and flowers. Cane and willow furniture is used exclusively ; there are no carpets, only rugs laid on the marble tiles ; the chairs in the parlor are arranged in a hollow square ; there is no getting off in a corner, or *tete-a-tetes* in quiet nooks. The entrance is through a wide, high archway, which closes both by iron gratings and heavy doors. An attendant sits in this archway at all times, combining the services of guard and porter. The bright interior, amounting many times to even luxuriousness, sets one to wondering as to the inmates and how they appear at home. This is hard to know, but one day I did—I called by mistake at the wrong door—the old colored servant could not be made to understand, and went back and forth to some one inside, and finally that some one had to come and direct me where to go; there came from the innermost recesses of that court to the grating door, a woman in the white, airy costume of the land, a perfect vision of beauty, tall, and shaped like a Venus, with a fortune of raven black hair, eyes that sparkled when she spoke, with a voice of exquisite loveliness, if I could I would have insisted that I was then at the house I was hunting for, but I had to go, and after that in my dreams I was a Spanish cavalier and serenaded beneath her casement—but I only do this in dreams. The lady's direction was correct, and I found my man, but had time to glance quickly at a Cuban residence.

The family carriage and coupé are kept in the archway that leads from the street, but the horses in the rear of the court. In the center of the court was a playing fountain with rich flowers blooming under its sprinkling waters; all around this court were wide galleries whence came the song of birds, and onto these galleries opened the family rooms—marble floors everywhere—the grand saloon parlor walls were hung with rich paintings, on the marble tiles were oriental rugs, in the center a large one, about which the light fancy-wood chairs were placed in a hollow square. There was every evidence of luxurious ease within, but outside, the low walls might be taken for such as inclose a warehouse or cotton yard. But when one comes to the

THE PATIO OF A CUBAN RESIDENCE.

SUBURBS OF HAVANA,

then does the ideal tropic home come to view in all its luxurious loveliness. The Captain-General has a summer residence in the suburbs where he resides from May to December, and the drive there is especially fine. While you are inspecting these villas drive to Vedado, the Cerro and Tulipan, the fashionable residence districts, and after these, extend the ride to the beautiful

CITY OF THE DEAD.

The Cemetery is usually the last place you drive to, but I will bring it in here as one of pleasure, seeing there is to be no procession. The entrance to the Cemetery and the Chapel within the gates, are the most exquisite pieces of architecture of the kind to be found anywhere, and the whole cemetery is filled with tombs, monuments and statues that would adorn a Greenwood or a Spring Grove. The grounds are located on the hills west of the City, and besides the local beauty of the place command a fine view of the island and the sea.

When one has seen Havana it is not all of Cuba by any means. The tourist, in justice to his own pleasure must do

CUBA BY RAIL.

First the suburban railways, a "dummy" train leaves from the sea front near La Punta and runs along the shore to the suburbs and extends to the cemetery.

The Marianao Railway extends west from Havana fifteen miles to Marianao (*Marry-ah-now*), a pretty little city of over 5,000 people, where there is a fine beach and excellent bathing, and near which is the famous Toledo sugar plantations, that may be visited by securing a permit from the manager in Havana.

The suburbs of Tulipan, Cerro, Ceiba, Buena Vista and Quemados, are all reached by the Marianao Railway.

La Prueba Railway and a branch of the Bahia Railway lead to the city of Guanabacoa six miles east of Havana, cross by ferry to Regla, thence trains run half hourly. Guanabacoa is one of the oldest towns in Cuba and has a population of 42,000. One of the places of interest to visit is the garden "Las Delicias," a private garden, planted for the amusement and pleasure of its owner—strangers are always welcome. Cut flowers and plants may be bought, and there are all kinds known to the tropics. On the commutation trains between Havana and Guanabacoa you may buy a brass check instead of a ticket, drop it in a box, pass through a turnstile and get on board. There are no conductors.

The station of the

BAHIA RAILWAY,

in Havana is at the Muelle de Luz, from whence passengers cross in ferry boats not unlike those in New York to Regla, where there is a nice station from which trains leave for eastern points in Cuba, and the ride is a most attractive one—the full name of the road is "Ferro-carril de la Bahia de la Habana," meaning literally the "Railway of the Bay of Havana," and my notes say good track, good cars and fast time, and if I remember right a seat on the left hand side is the best—but on both sides there is much to see, the road runs through a rich valley with rolling hills covered with palms and cocoa trees on each side, rising to high mountains that lift up in fantastic shapes like old Polonius' clouds in Hamlet, like a camel, or backed like a weasel, or like a whale—or like the old man of the mountains in Catskills, all blue in the distance sometimes and sometimes near at hand. Near the road are the low thatched houses of the country people, built of palm logs, thatched with palm leaves and weather-boarded with palm bark, with here and there the white house of the planter's home or that of his manager.

The train makes fast time and comes to the stations in rapid succession, stopping at each one, and before it starts a Chinaman stands on the platform and rings a dinner-bell which is the Cuban for "all aboard." This same Chinaman acts as train-boy and passes through the cars offering guava jelly and native cheese spread on plantain leaves, but no morning papers or yellow-back novels. When the whistle sounds for

MATANZAS,

a seat on the left will show the best view of the city, and, on the high hill beyond, the church of Montserat which overlooks the valley of the Yumuri, which with the caves of Bella Mar form the chief attractions.

The railway station at Matanzas is a fine building, and a much nicer station than is usually found in towns of the same size in America ; by-the-way, you will read the signs in Cuba and may not know what they mean, "*Boletines*" is over the ticket office, "*Equipages*" over the baggage-room, "*Señoras*" is over the door to the ladies' room and *Señores* over that for gentlemen. Tickets are shown on entering the station at Havana, punched by the conductor and taken up by the gateman at Matanzas.

Matanzas is eighty-five miles from Havana, located on the bay at the junction of the San Juan and Yumuri rivers, a city of the pure Cuban type, with narrow streets opening into plazas, low buildings, luxuriant trees and gardens and good hotels withal.   One goes to Matanzas to see the caves and the

VALLEY OF THE YUMURI.

The journey may be made from Havana and return to that city in a day, allowing time to visit the valley and the caves. A longer stay is desirable, but the average

VALLEY OF THE YUMURI, FROM MONTSERAT CHURCH.

American is in a hurry and this story is written to suit him. Consult the schedules of the railways without relying on this, for schedules change sometimes, even in Cuba.

Interpreters of the various hotels meet the trains on arrival at Matanzas, and will secure the volantas while you are at breakfast or securing rooms. The volanta is the easiest riding vehicle in the world ; it rests on two wheels, the body of the volanta suspended on leather throughbraces, like a stage-coach, long shafts of elastic wood connects with the horse ; another horse, ridden by the driver, is attached outside the shafts ; with this rig a ride over the hills of Cuba is the event of a lifetime. The horses start off at a full trot, and keep it up all the way, up hill and down. Leaving the hotel the route is through the city, past the Plaza, the Palace, and the Casino, then through long narrow streets of low houses to the hills outside the city, where a long, white road leads to the highest, on the top of which is the Church of Montserat overlooking the beautiful valley, than which there is no more lovelier in all my world of travels ; it is worth all the journey to Cuba to go and look at it. One does not drive through the valley, but to the hills that hedge it in, and enjoys the enchantment that distance lends.

The church stands on the top of the hill, and but for the stone walls that surround it one might fall and roll down the steep sides hundreds of feet ; far below the little Yumuri river runs, no bigger than a brook, the white road winds about through the palms and up the hills on the other side ; looking from the east wall the city of Matanzas is in the near distance, the bay beyond, and further on the hills where the caves are.

The Church of Montserat enjoys the fame of many miracles, and the grateful pilgrims who have sojourned here and been cured are numbered in legions ; you may purchase a charm or relic at Montserat that may have a talismanic effect on your future fortunes. The church is a not imposing structure, of a greenish hue, built of stone, surmounted by a cross ; in front, under the trees, are four statues with the inscriptions—Ledida, Taragona, Barcelona, and Gerona ; inside are glass cases containing relics and offerings made by pilgrims ; on the walls are curious pictures, one depicts the wreck of a passenger train, the cars rolling down an embankment, reminding the traveler of the uncertainties of life even on the best regulated railways.

This is one of the places it is hard to get away from, but if we go back to Havana this afternoon, we must hurry on to the

CAVES OF BELLA MAR.

The route is back through the city again, but by different streets ; passing over a bridge across the St. John, the road comes to the sea shore, skirting the bay and passing some beautiful suburban residences and the local summer resorts—then climbs the hills about three miles to where the caves are. I do not know whether

MAZZANTINI.

the boundaries of the infernal regions come nearer the earth's surface at any one place, but if they do, it must be near Bella Mar, and the caves may be a disused side-entrance—the weather in the caves is of that summer nature to make one ask questions. Ladies, remove your wraps, leave them at the entrance. Gentlemen, the ladies will excuse you, take off your coats, and unless your collar is celluloid, or you have an extra one, divest yourself of that too—because its warm enough for you down-stairs—but withal a wonderful under-ground journey.

Guides with torches precede you down a flight of stairs—thence on for a mile or so it is easy walking, through lofty chambers, dazzling in their deco-rations, ceilings hung with glittering stalactites varying in size from my lady's finger to tons in weight, and like diamonds reflecting from their crystals a thousand hues—these are in fantastic shapes, some from their re-semblances have acquired names—there is a "Mantle of Columbus;" a "Guardian Spirit;" and a piano composed of a series of small stalactites of different lengths, which on being struck, give forth a melo-dious chord. There is a "Monkey Sa-lon," suggesting a convention of frozen monkeys, evidently not frozen in the cave though. There is a pool of water called the "Baño de la Inglesa," from the fact that an English lady tourist once bathed in its waters. The caves have never been fully explored; there are other chambers —at a point on the route is an opening, where a stone being thrown can be heard bounding from side to side till the sound is lost in the distance; and the guides say they never have gone as far as it is possible through the different openings—it is a mam-moth cave that will compare with Kentucky's Mammoth or Virginia's Luray.

Now those who wish may return to Havana, and those who wish proceed to

CARDENAS,

"GUERRITA."

the very youngest city in Cuba, and its growth is something wonderful, there are now nearly 25,000 people. The city is located on a fine bay and is backed by a most

fertile country, and contains a sugar refinery and other manufacturing interests. The train which leaves Regla (opposite Havana) in the morning, arrives at Cardenas about noon, a fast train over a good road and passing through a country totally unlike any other I ever saw; a country of rolling hills with fertile sugar valleys in between, high mountains, not in long continuous ranges, but sharp abrupt peaks whose sides appear almost perpendicular. Cardenas is the first city in Cuba to erect a statue to Columbus. This, perhaps, because the ashes gave out. So many cities could not have ashes and so Cardenas must have a statue. The journey by rail may be continued on through middle Cuba to Santo Domingo, Sagua, Santa Clara and to Cienfuegos, either of which cities may be reached by a twelve hours' daylight ride, that will show the American tourist more newness than he can get in any twelve in his own country. Starting from Havana on morning trains of either the Bahia or Havana Railroads, arrival can be made at either of the places before nightfall.

The railway system of Cuba extends over the central portion of the island, traversing the fertile interior, touching the northern coast at Havana, Matanzas, Cardenas and Concha, and the southern shore at Batabano and Cienfuegos.

La Linea de la Compania de Caminos de Hierro de la Habana is a long name, meaning

THE HAVANA RAILWAY.

The road starts from *Villa Nueva* station, Havana, runs eastward to Matanzas and Union, connecting there with other lines for interior and coast cities. It is a fine railway, and well equipped. Tourists, who have not time for further rail journeys, should go over one line to Matanzas and return by the other. This company has a line west from Havana to Guanajay and southward to

BATABANO AND THE SOUTH COAST,

crossing the island at one of the narrowest parts, being only thirty-one miles. The run from Havana is made in one hour and twenty minutes; pretty good time, considering the ten stops and the slow entrance to Havana, where it is required that a man on horseback must ride between the rails in front of the engine from the limits to Villa Nueva, the city station. Batabano is the port where the steamships sail for Santiago de Cuba, The Isle of Pines, Vuelta-Abajo and other ports on the south coast on regular days, which change sometimes and the sailing dates will not be written down.

The Isle of Pines is about seventy-five miles from Batabano, and requires about eight hours' sail. Trains leave Havana in the morning, arriving at Batabano an hour and a half later, arriving per steamer at the Isle of Pines in the afternoon. The island is noted principally for its fine woods—mahogany, red-wood, ebony, rosewood and other valuable timbers; pines, of course, hence its name. It is truly the most tropical place within easy American reach; all tropical birds, animals and reptiles abound in the forests. There are mineral springs on the island which enjoy a local reputation for their curative qualities. From the Isle of Pines also comes a valuable marble in various colors. Altogether, a most interesting tour to make.

SANTIAGO DE CUBA

is the chief city of eastern Cuba, and is the capital of the State of Santiago de Cuba, and, of course, the residence of the civil governor and the church functionaries, located on the south shore on one of the finest bays, in the midst of a fine coffee and sugar region, for which it is the shipping point. Near Santiago are also the celebrated iron ore beds and copper mines, most favorably known for their excellent qualities; ores which are shipped to the United States and other parts of the world.

The metal deposits are pronounced very rich and are attracting the attention of our capitalists. The mines are worked now by native companies, but not to their fullest capacity nor to the best advantage.

As yet, Santiago de Cuba cannot be reached by rail from Havana; the tourist for that point must sail from Batabano, Cienfuegos or from Havana and around the island.

The line running west from Havana is called the

FERRO-CARRIL DEL OESTE.

Trains leave Cristina station, Havana, in the morning, and returning in the

SANTIAGO DE CUBA.

evening, give the hurrying American time to make the tour in a day, and travel through the famous

TOBACCO REGIONS.

It is a curious fact that all the finest tobacco in the world should be grown in so small a country as Cuba, but still more curious that it should be confined to so small a portion of that country—and it is well worth while to make the little trip necessary, to see where grows the weed the fragrance of whose blue smoke is the delight and talk and solace of two hemispheres.

Morning trains from Havana connect at Paso Real with stages and volantas for the mineral springs and baths of San Diego de los Baños, noted for wonderful cures of rheumatism, paralysis and diseases of the blood. The resort is called the Cuban Saratoga, and is largely patronized by wealthy natives both for health and pleasure;

there are ample hotel accommodations.   The stage or volanta ride is only nine miles from Paso Real on the main line of the West Railroad.

The scenery along the line is lovely in the extreme and the added attractions of the tobacco regions gives another subject to talk on at home—you can tell them you saw where the cigars grow. .

It will be of interest to note these

POINTERS ON CUBAN RAILWAY TRAVEL.

The different railways publish folders or time cards in Spanish, but it is easy to understand them—the names of stations of course are the same in English so are the time figures, then it is only necessary to know that *mañana* means morning and *tarde,* afternoon ; *tarifa* is the tariff and *precios* the price of tickets, both terms being used;— *hora* is the hour and *minutos* the minutes ; *trenes* means the trains and *linea* the line ; now take the folder and read it, the lesson is easy.

There are first, second and third class cars with a different rate of fare for each car, for instance, the first class fare from Havana to Matanzas is $4.25; 2d, $3.00 and 3d, $1.75.

Tickets must be purchased before entering the cars, conductors punch the tickets but do not take them up, the agent at destination does that.

On all the main lines there are good accommodations, the track is good, and trains make fast time.   The following are some rules in force :

The sale of tickets will be closed five minutes before departure of trains.

Tickets only good for date stamped on.

Babies free.

Children to 7 years old will pay half-fare, employees to decide the age.   A child without a ticket will pay full-fare.

Passengers must show their tickets as many times as so exacted by the conductor.

Passengers without tickets will pay one-third additional for first tract, and the total afterwards, from point of departure.

If trains do not arrive on time passengers can desist from their trip, price of tickets being refunded.

Employees of the train can eject passengers without tickets, unwilling to pay their fare, or behaving improperly, and in case of resistance to be delivered to the authorities.

Passengers losing a ticket must pay its price till justification of loss.

Passengers are only allowed, free, a hat-box, valise or satchel 24 inches long, by 12 wide and 9 high.   All other baggage to go in the baggage-car paying freight.

Traveling on the platforms strictly prohibited.

No animals allowed on the first-class car, except fighting-cocks in their baskets.

In other cars, muzzled dogs and six chickens are tolerated, paying freight.

Firearms, to go in the baggage-room.

No colored persons allowed in the first-class cars.

No packages allowed containing fish or ice in such a state as to annoy passengers.

The delivery of baggage will be made upon presentation of the check by order of numbers.

$50 will be paid for a trunk lost, $20 for a valise or satchel, and hat-boxes $4.

The fractions of money will be charged as wholes by the Company.

THE MANNERS AND CUSTOMS

of the Cubans are in many cases peculiar, but always pleasing.   They have main tained a good name for the courtesies and kindness to strangers.   If you admire anything that belongs to a Cuban he says it is at your service ; if you call at his house, he says in his words of welcome, "this house is yours;" but it would hardly be proper to ask him to make out the deeds till you call again.

Cuban ladies possess a beauty above the average pretty woman, and are modest withal. They do not go out alone or receive gentlemen unless in the presence of a duenna or older member of the family—'tis well—for it always seemed to me that those great black eyes and long lashes, drooping on pretty cheeks with such lips as theirs, could do a world of mischief, and if left alone and untrammeled break up whole families. Their costumes are most bewitching, all light and airy. They wear no hats or bonnets, but instead, the lace mantilla, hanging in graceful folds from their inky hair—a black mantilla for the street and a white one for the theatre—bless 'em for that one fact alone—no hats at the theatre. The milliner's is an undiscovered art in Cuba, and she would starve to death if she depended on the patronage of the ladies there.

I have often wondered how a Cuban lover ever got a chance to say his pretty talks and tell his sweetheart what was his opinion of her ; but when I went to a ball and saw the "*Danza,*" I ceased to wonder. In the maneuvers of that slow and peculiar dance he has the best chance in the world—a man can't dance the *Danza* with but one woman at a time, and the *Danza* is danced by the hour. I think its duration is only measured by the endurance of the musicians. The *Danza* is not a polka, nor a schottische ; more of a waltz, with the time and steps divided by about eight ; it is hardly even a dance, but a slow walk around, and though not fatiguing, with frequent stoppages—I think not to rest, but to talk. The positions of the dancers are the same as in a waltz, and give ample opportunity for extended embraces to slow music, and here it is that I have figured it out that the Cuban lover has his opportunity.

The fêtes and balls are largely attended and the people seem to devote their energies to complete enjoyment, and they last till the sunshine dims the gaslight. The people go to church early in the morning but the balance of the day is devoted to pleasure.

The ladies go shopping on wheels, and do not, as a general thing, get out of the carriage at the stores, the goods being brought out for their inspection, and if satisfactory, the goods are taken home and, I suppose, the bill sent to *padre.*

Business men take coffee at home in the morning, breakfast down-town about our lunch time, and dine at home after business hours ; it sounds queer to go into an office at noon and be told the party inquired for has gone to breakfast.

On account of the climate, I suppose, nobody seems in a hurry in Cuba, and many people look tired ; I saw a cart backed up to a front door, it was loaded with brick, a negro piled up four bricks in the end of the cart and waited for a Chinaman to carry them in, and thus after a while unloaded his cart. I suppose some man in the back yard (like Paddy's man at the top of the scaffold, where he carried bricks) did all the work. The average costume of the laborer is a knit shirt and a pair of overalls, whether it's December or May.

Everything goes in and out the front door of a Havana house. Marketing goes in and garbage goes out. Horses and carriages use the same entrance the guests do.

Horses carry instead of draw their burdens. If you see green objects coming down the street, don't imagine that "Burnham wood has come to Dunsinane." There are little horses under those piles of green fodder.

I saw tandem teams of eight horses and donkeys to one two-wheeled cart. Mules and horses wear heavy woolen head-dresses of tassels as protection against the sun, and oxen wear their yokes on the back of their heads just aft the horn, and some of them do business as switch engines in the depot yards.

People get "broke" in Cuba just as they do here at home, perhaps more so, as the Government undertakes to do the pawnbroker's business, so if you have anything to put up the Queen of Spain will act as your uncle, or more properly, your aunt. Money would seem hard to get in Cuba, and also that many people desire to get it, as it is common to see armed soldiers in the entry and corridors of the bank—but perhaps they are only there to look after the cashiers—that would be a good idea in some American banks, and likely reduce the tide of travel to Canada.

To tell all of the manners and customs of these good people would make a very large book of interesting reading, and these are only notes taken at random during a flying visit to the Island in the season of '87-8, and are written for the information of those who may contemplate the most delightful voyage, and with the wish that their experiences may be as prolific of pleasant memories as was my visit to the beautiful Queen of the Antilles.

SANITARY.

To assure the timid and satisfy any inquiry on the subject, it is proper to note here the sanitary regulations prescribed by the Board of Health, and scrupulously observed on board the steamers of the Plant Line. An investigation of the channel of introduction of yellow fever into Florida was ordered and a committee of the Board of Health sent to Tampa, Key West and Havana. The report was in every way favorable to the line, and no evidence adduced tending to any sort of foundation for anything said against it by uninformed rumor.

The following are extracts from the Official Report:

"'The vessels of this line are the 'Mascotte' and 'Olivette,' both new iron vessels, constructed on the most approved principles and adapted especially for the Gulf trade. While these ships are marvels of beauty and elegance, they are also marvels in the way of ventilation and improved sanitary arrangements. In fine, they were built to meet the requirements of West Indian transportation. They ply, as you know, between Havana and Tampa, touching at Key West.

That you may understand the precautionary measures adopted by this line for the prevention of the introduction of yellow fever, we will state in substance the regulations which are in force from May 10 to November 1, which regulations are subject to such additional regulations from time to time as may be deemed advisable or necessary:

1st. The officers and crews of both vessels of this line shall be acclimated to the island of Cuba, thus rendering them practically exempt from yellow fever.

2d. Every steamship of the line shall enter the harbor of Havana only after sunrise, and shall leave the port before sunset of the same day. While in Havana each vessel shall be anchored or moored in the eastern portion of the bay, which is to the windward of the city, the prevailing winds being from the northeast.

3d. The vessels shall hold no communication with the shore at Havana except upon the written permission of Dr. D. M. Burgess. All officers of the vessel and members of the crew are forbidden to go on shore or on board any other vessel except upon the written permission of Dr. Burgess. Nor shall any person from the shore visit any vessel of the line, except upon such permission. This regulation shall likewise apply to Key West should the necessity arise.

4th. The agents of this line at Havana will require from every person desiring to take passage, as a prerequisite to obtaining such passage, a certificate from Dr. Burgess stating that such person has given satisfactory evidence of having had yellow fever or being acclimated to the island of Cuba or neighboring islands, also that such person comes from a healthy locality.

5th. Should any case of fever develop on any vessel of the line after leaving

Havana, it shall be the duty of the captain to promptly report the same to the health officer of the port next reached, *i. e.,* Key West or Tampa. Such case shall be considered yellow fever until disproved. All contaminated bedding and clothes shall be considered infectious and subject to such orders as the health officer may direct.

6th. After leaving port, the hatches shall be opened as soon as practicable, and a wind-sail set that the ship's interior may be thoroughly ventilated. The U. S. mails and all baggage to be fumigated in air-tight compartments as directed by Drs. Burgess, Porter and Wall.

7th. The vessels shall be thoroughly cleansed twice a week at Tampa. All bilge water shall be removed by pumping and sponging. The bilge space after being thoroughly cleansed, shall be treated alternately with bi-chloride of mercury and chloride of lime. Particular attention shall be given water-closets and waste-pipes of all kinds that no offensive odors shall exist.

8th. Drs. Burgess and Wall will make a personal inspection of every portion of each vessel upon its arrival at Havana or Tampa. Likewise an inspection of passengers, officers and crew.

9th. The bill of health of each vessel on each trip, shall state clearly and distinctly whether or not the above requirements have been complied with.

Having heard these regulations, two questions are naturally suggested. 1st. Are these rules sufficiently effective and can they be carried out? 2d. Will they be carried out? After a careful investigation we are assured of the practical working of the above regulations.

In consideration of these facts we believe that commerce with the West Indies is not only possible, but may be, with safety, maintained during the summer, without the restrictions of the old system of quarantine."

AROUND THE CORNER.

That part of this country known as Florida has been, not inaptly, called "the corner of the continent," and if it *is* the corner, the title chosen for a sketch of a trip to Cuba may be as aptly chosen as *around* that corner.

That Columbus discovered America, as taught for generations, with an occasional dissenter placing the point of discovery further north and changing the name of the discoverer, is a memory of schooldays, and this history need not extend thereto. Suffice it to say that Columbus went home and told a tale of the land which started an excursion business that has lived, with some interruptions, through nearly four centuries. Ponce de Leon was the first excursionist of note. He came, not in a special car, as do noted tourists of to-day, but in his own ship, made a longer voyage with the same ulterior object—the finding the fountain of health. The ancient mariner and original excursionist may have believed too implicitly in the stories he had heard, and expected to find a too material spring, whose waters were a preventive of wrinkles, possessed a smoothing quality and a power to effect a bloom of perpetual youth; but whatever he *had* heard was not far away from the reports of to-day. Only, people of this age are not given to reading too literally, but with due credence are attracted thither to the same land which Ponce de Leon had heard was the panacea for his growing old, and follow where he led the way, more than three hundred years ago. De Soto was another original tourist. His landing was at Tampa, and the hunt, not for the health-renewing waters, but gold and plunder, was pursued northward. Now the point of debarkation is at the northern border, and the pursuit to the southward through the Flowery State, embarking at De Soto's landing for the India Isles and a still warmer clime.

Physically, Cuba belongs to our domain—belongs to the domain of the tourist —at least since it has been shown that it only requires a ferry-boat to cross over.

Politically, the Island is His Majesty's, of Spain ; but the little king, through his gracious mother, the Queen Regent, welcomes the great American traveler to the hills and valleys of this island of perpetual summer.   To all intents and purposes, the opening of a line from her chief port on the Gulf coast to Havana, is but increasing Florida's territory of pleasure travel, and those who have been disposed to carp at what seemed to them opposition attractions, have not regarded the fact that the tour "around the corner" may bring back some who thought they had done the State long ago, and some new ones who, but for the addition of the Cuban feature, may not have traveled thitherward at all.

It was the intention to say nothing in this about the unanimous direction of all roads toward Rome, but the location of Jacksonville, and the geographical direction of all railways to the southeast corner of the continent, and centering as they do at Jacksonville, makes the temptation to use the quotation hardly to be resisted.

Coming down the coast from New York by all lines via Charleston and Savannah, Augusta and Aiken ; from the north via Cincinnati and Louisville ; from the northwest via Chicago and St. Louis ; from the southwest via New Orleans and Mobile, there are long lines of Pullman cars that have their terminus at Jacksonville, whose passengers need not leave their places from departure to destination, and on certain trains till they step on board ship to sail for Cuba ; hence the journey has naught of the old-time material for unpleasant memories.

The monotony of the longer sea voyage of other days may be broken on this route by pleasant

STOPPING PLACES BY THE WAY.

Charleston—with its historic memories of the war, its marks of earthquake misfortunes.   The beautiful gardens, and the harbor with its forts and batteries are all attractive, in themselves sufficient for the request of a stop-over ticket.   The old palace-looking Charleston Hotel, with its heavy pillared colonnade, is a reminiscence of the hotel architecture of old days ; but the living there is of modern excellence, and also at the Pavilion and Waverly.

Asheville—noted for its climatic advantage and scenic beauty and its Battery Park and Swannanoa hotels.   Aiken—for its hotel of comfort at Highland Park, the pineries and healthful sunshine.   Augusta—for its beautiful streets and suburbs. Savannah—for its parks and moss-hung trees—where the tourist from the East may break his journey, find much to interest, and good living withal.

If the journey is from central North, at Chattanooga is grand old Lookout, with its battle-field "above the clouds," and a hundred others on the routes to Atlanta, the "gate city of the South"—where always the traveler is welcome and made to feel the hospitality of a genial people.   Macon is on the borders of the pine lands, set upon the hills in the centre of the Empire State of the South.   Thomasville, noted far and wide, the favorite of the health searcher and those on pleasure bent, a veritable "Yankee Paradise," where the balmy breezes come in zephyrs, aroma-laden, from the purring pines bearing health and new life on every breath. Besides the wonderful health-giving climate of Thomasville, the very excellent hotels of that resort are attractions within themselves.   The Mitchell House is one of *the* resort hotels of the country, not excelled even at the great summer watering-places. The Piney Woods Hotel, located in a grove of pines that localizes the *sobriquet* of "Yankee Paradise."   There are a score or more of other hotels, not equal in size to these, but there is good living.   Tallahassee, the city of roses, which came by its name by Divine right in the crowning of its chocolate hills luxuriantly with the queen of all the flowers.   There is mention of Tally-ho line from Metcalf, a station on the Thomasville and Monticello Railway.   This ride through pines, over the smooth

roads of white sand, is one full of interest and pleasurable novelty. The hotels of Tallahassee are up to the standard.

All these towns and cities are on the line, and more there are down the peninsula, where stops may be made on this new route to Cuba.

Jacksonville, the metropolis of the State, is the terminus of the through car lines and the great distributing point for all Florida. Everybody stops at Jacksonville either going or returning, some a longer time, as the fine city has attractions in the fashionable hotels, fine drives, and sails on the broad river; excursions to the sea at Pablo or Mayport, by rail or sail, or by steamer up the river of abundant waters, the wide St. John's. And all the rest of it, that goes to make a delightful sojourn at a fashionable watering place. All that may be remembered of summer days at Saratoga or Bar Harbor can be found at Jacksonville, from the excellence of the hotels to the frivolities of the life therein. There is at Jacksonville a hotel kept by a man whose only standard is that of superior excellence—a host who has the patronage of the best people and caters to it by keeping a hotel whose title, the proprietor says, must be "The Best." The Windsor is the hotel and Orvis the man. The St. James, the Everett, the Carleton, are all in the front rank of resort hotels, with many others above the average.

I say sleeping-car "runs" end at Jacksonville. For the most part they do, but if the journey to Cuba is to be made without a stop, there is a Pullman which does not stop at Jacksonville, but extends its "run" to Tampa and on to the pier at Port Tampa, alongside the "Mascotte" and "Olivette," the ships of the ferry.

Leisurely travelers can find many places south of Jacksonville where to make pleasant breaks in their journeys. At St. Augustine one may have a foretaste of the old Spanish scenes to be visited at the end of the voyage, and a visit to the oldest city in this country is fraught with many pleasures.

All the world has heard of the famous Ponce de Leon, a replica of some old Moorish castle, as it looks to be, with its turrets and towers, court-yards and gateways, a picture taken from the ancient history of lordly Spain. This, with the Alcazar, and Cordova, and the other hostelries of more modern build, the San Marco, Magnolia, Florida, are the names which insure good living while stealing some days from another century.

St. Augustine does not seem to grasp the newness of advancing ages, and she is all the more attractive because she does not. As far back as extends the memory of the oldest inhabitant, the newspaper writer and guide-book scribe has written it "ye ancient citye"—till it has been questioned whether St. Augustine ever was new. As the town is old so everything in it is—it is the *old* fort, and it was the *old* Sergeant, now gone to his rest, that showed its old dungeons, casements, parapets, towers, prison cells and subterranean passages, and told his old, old story of mysteries that rivaled the Inquisition, which may or may not have occurred, and which he was never certain of, as he (though old himself) "was not there and didn't see it," and of course could not speak positively on hearsay. When the old Sergeant told of the King of Spain's (alleged) looking wistfully westward over the seas, some three hundred years ago, and saying that he was looking to see the towers of the castle of San Marco, which must be mountain high (not mounting high ; the ancient Kings of Spain never perniciously played upon words), which had cost so much money and so many men and years to build, he, the old Sergeant, always told the anecdote with inevitable interpolation of the hint that he was not present, and of course did not hear the king say anything about the old fort at all—somebody else had told him about it.

All the balance of this great country owes a debt of gratitude to St. Augustine in that, that old city saved the country from an everlasting "whitewash" in securing to it the only "old ruins" in the whole country, and the native points with pardonable pride to the crumbling walls of San Marco, of Fort Mantanzas, the City Gates and scores of low-walled houses in veritable proof of the city's claims.

The sea wall is not new. It is old to many lovers, whose walks up and down have worn smooth the cap-stones. The pyramidal tombs of Major Dade and his massacred men are moss-covered with age, and of a build that is Egyptian in its style. In the old cemeteries the tumble-down tombs show more 16's and 17's than of 18's in naming the centuries of the dates of departure of the Dons and Donas who rest beneath them.

The streets of St. Augustine are as old as the town is, and a great deal narrower, too narrow for practical purposes, but wide enough for St. Augustine, yet narrow enough to provide two shady sides all day long, even with the low, one-storied houses. What more could be desired of a street in a town as old as St. Augustine ?

With all its oldness St. Augustine is to have in the near future the newest thing on wheels, a vestibuled train service, which will cross the St. John's at Palatka or Jacksonville or both.

This old town is not on the beaten track to Cuba, and the trip there is a slight divergence, but the main line is not an hour out of the way. The line of railway down on the west side of the St. John's passes through Magnolia and Green Cove Springs, both noted health resorts, where the baths of curative waters are, and whose fame has gone abroad throughout the land. Palatka, rejoicing in the pretty title of the Gem City and its possession of such a hotel as the Putnam House, is a distributing point for the central peninsula and a most pleasant place withal, where 'tis good to stop for rest and pleasure, and during the stay, tour the mystic, crooked waters of the romantic Ocklawaha and gaze deep down in the depths of the silvery waters of Silver Spring, or "branch off" to the beautiful lake region of the western part of the peninsula, or to the lower eastern coast at Daytona, and come to the main line again, which follows the eastern shore of the St. Johns, and crosses that river at its juntion with Lake Monroe, and comes to Sanford.

If there is time for yet other tours in the Flowery State, Sanford is the stopping place for that of the Indian river, and no other is more attractive, leading as it does through the more tropical regions where palms and palmettos make the forests, and oranges and bananas the cultivated grounds and gardens.

The straight way of the through route of the Pullman from New York is a little to the southwest from Sanford ; leaving that charming city by the lake the track is up grade, more than would be supposed in such an apparently level country ; at an elevation of 250 feet and only 35 miles from the sea, crosses the back-bone of the peninsula and rolls down on the western slope to the Gulf of Mexico. Passing en route, the garden of the land, a very park of intervening lakes, groves, gardens and pines, broken here and there by bustling cities in miniature with extending suburbs that grow to villages and towns further down—where, at any one a stop may be made, but the sleeper hurries on to Tampa where the ship is waiting.

TAMPA.

It has been more than three hundred years since Panfilo de Narvaez sailed the first ship into the waters of Tampa Bay, and ever since he came, and De Soto after him, the returning tourist has brought back wonderful tales of its beauties, and told fish stories that must sound improbable to any one who has never been a-fishing at Tampa. The editor of the *New York Journal of Commerce* says that for a day's fishing no one need go further than an hour's rowing from the wharf at Tampa. Even the amateur angler can come home before the day is out, simply tired out catching the fish. It is no weary tramp through the woods or tedious sail to where the fish are ; they are right at Tampa, at the wharf. So much for the sport. What else ?

There is being erected at Tampa a hotel which, in its magnificent proportions and appointments, will rival any building of its kind in the country.

Tampa's new hotel will be the first tourist hotel in the United States, and, so far as known, is the first in the world to be built entirely fire-proof—all the walls, partitions, floors and ceilings being of brick and concrete, and all the beams of rolled steel.

The hotel company, after many delays, succeeded in purchasing about thirty acres of land fronting the river opposite the city, and built a draw-bridge connecting the hotel grounds with the city of Tampa.

The grounds overlook Tampa Bay, the city and Fort Brook. From the towers may be seen the waters of the Gulf of Mexico, twenty miles away. In the lawns and gardens are the trees of the South, great oaks, orange trees and the wild lemon, with their fragrant blossoms ; the magnolia and the roses will also lend their perfumes. On the grounds are springs of mineral waters—chalybeate and sulphur.

The portion of the hotel now being constructed is 555 feet long, from north to south, varying in width from 50 to 100 feet, and four stories high. To this will be added the large dining-room, the plan being in the form of a Greek cross with windows on ten sides and surmounted with a dome. The smaller dining-rooms, billiard-room, storerooms, kitchens, and servants' quarters will all be in buildings separate from the hotel and all fire-proof.

The architecture is adapted from the land of the Saracens. The horseshoe arch and star and crescent meet the eye at every turn. Four corners of the whole structure are guarded by round towers, surmounted with swelled domes, and four more towers at the angles of the centre building will be surmounted with minarets suggestive of the Mazurin and his admonition that " there is no God but Allah, and Mahomet is his prophet." The roofs are flat, with long horizontal lines only slightly broken, after the custom of the Orient.

The principal floor is elevated six feet above the grade, and the lawn slopes gradually from the house to the river bank.

The house fronts alike east and west, and has spacious and elaborately ornamented verandas on both sides. The dining-rooms are at the end of main building, hence no back rooms or rooms into which the sun's unbroken rays cannot penetrate. Portions of the veranda extend up two stories, under which are small balconies connecting with the rooms behind them ; other portions of the veranda are extended outward, circular in form, and covered with spherical domes, surmounted with lanterns.

The dining-room and the ball-room are each built semi-circular at their extreme ends, surmounted with domes, and surrounded with verandas on three sides each, the

AN INCIDENT OF
MEXICAN BRIGAND LIFE.

"El salto de Juan Medina"
(The leap of Juan Medina)

floors of which are level with the floors of the apartments, with windows six feet wide opening to the floor, without any obstructions of any kind. The verandas will also be extended and form two *port cocheres*, one to accommodate carriages, the other to be used by the cars that will convey passengers to and from the railroad station.

The exterior walls are of dark red bricks, with buff and red brick arches and stone sill and belt courses. The cornices will be principally of stone and iron, the piazza columns of steel supported on piers of cut stone imported from the British West India Islands.

The main entrances are alike on the east and west fronts, and on each through three pairs of double doors ; the doorways are guarded by sixteen polished granite columns supporting Moorish arches, over which are balconies opening from the gallery around the rotunda at the second floor.

The rotunda is about seventy-five feet square, two stories high, and has two rows of coupled polished granite columns. The corridors vary in width from eleven to eighteen feet. The drawing-room, which is forty by seventy-five feet, and the writing and reading rooms, are separated from the rotunda and corridors by single plate glasses, eight feet wide, and reaching from floor to ceilings, opposite which are mirrors of the same size.

The principal staircases will be of iron. Passenger and baggage elevators, steam-heat, open wood fireplaces, electric lights, and all the latest improvements will be introduced.

The rooms are arranged in suites and single, with a private bath to about every three rooms. Nearly every room has a fireplace and large clothes-room.

There are sixteen suites containing double parlors, nineteen by twenty-four feet each, with three bedrooms and two baths; some are arranged with private halls on the "flat" plan. There are dozens of single parlors with one or more bedrooms and baths attached. Other rooms have long windows, private piazzas, balconies and circular niches, fifteen feet diameter, with windows in three sides.

All apartments on the first floor are connected with the corridor by arches six feet wide, thirteen feet high, the lower parts of which will be screened with ornamental cabinet work similar to that found in the palaces of Andalusia.

In finishing and furnishing the guests' parlors and rooms, there will be floors of marble tile, marquetry and of plain wood, and floors with mattings, carpets and rugs for those who prefer them, while the styles, material and colors of the furniture will be in as great variety.

No tourist hotel yet built has an equal extent of rotunda, parlors, reception-rooms, etc., etc., connected and appearing as one grand reception-hall, nor has any hotel yet introduced plate-glass screens and mirrors as liberally as they will be found here.

Spanish furniture and decorations from Barcelona and Cadiz will prevail in the drawing-rooms and parlors. Earthen ranges and full sets of Spanish culinary utensils will be introduced into the kitchen in addition to the so-called French ranges, and will be presided over by Spanish cooks.

If you will, Castilian food will be served, while the thrifty Catalonian will undertake to quench your thirst with anything from the water of a green cocoanut, tamorindo or orchatta to the incomparable wines of the realms of his infantile Majesty Alfonso XIII.

A Mexican band will discourse music while you dine in the only hotel in the United States that will or can serve a liberal variety of fresh vegetables every day throughout the winter to the total exclusion of canned products.

We have written a part of what we can learn about what is now being done. We might write more, and there is more to write about than we can write, but the architect does not see fit to disclose all the plans to anyone. The plans of the buildings are incomplete, although the building is nearly half finished. It becomes more expensive as it approaches completion.

Tampa is fast becoming a city of cigars, bidding to rival her neighbor Havana, as fine cigars being made as in that city. Prove this by your own smoking, and if you would extend the proof to friends at home, remember that the Southern Express will deliver a box to any part of the United States. There is no duty on Tampa cigars.

Tampa has some pages in the earliest history of the country, and is a place of legend and romance. The story of the Indian

KING HIRRIHIGUA'S DAUGHTER,

rivals that of Powhattan and Pocahontas; a prettier tale in itself, with a hero of a more romantic name than Smith. It was Juan Ortiz, whom the king made captive, and bethought him of a roast, Ortiz being young and tender; but being young and tender, Hirrihigua's daughter bethought her of sweeter uses for this young man;

argued the case with the old man, and finally persuaded him to desist from the intended dinner, and before the roast was even under-done, the pale-faced prisoner was
removed from the gridiron
of poles, and the Princess
ministered to him, and herself cared for his hurts.

This story does not end
as in a novel. The couple
thus met by chance, and,
under such adverse circumstances, did not marry and
become the progenitors of
so many first families as in
Virginia.

The King either got
hungry again, or repented
him of his mercy, and once
more condemned his pos-
sible son-in-law to death.
And yet, once more, the
Princess (the chronicler, by
some impious disregard of
modern curiosity, does not
give her name), came to
Ortiz's rescue. She told
Juan of her father's dire de-
cision, and told him to flee,
the narrator of the legend
says, "under the cover of
the darkness of night, and
guided him away herself into the forest, with a minute
direction how he should
reach one Mucoso, a chief,
who was her affianced lover.
This Mucoso appears to
have been a man God made
—a man rooted in honor.
He consented to protect
Ortiz; and, having once
undertaken, carried out his
word with fidelity under
temptations that would
have shaken a Christian
mightily. For it was not
long before Hirrihigua demanded the return of Ortiz.

A MEXICAN GIRL.

Mucoso refused. Hirrihigua put on the screws. Mucoso could not have his daughter unless he gave up the prisoner; still Mucoso refused. He refused to the end;
and to the end Hirrihigua's daughter upheld him in his refusal; and to the end this
savage man and woman, for pure honor, expended their love's happiness to save a
foreigner who had come to conquer them."

I do not say all this occurred in Tampa—like the old Sergeant (of most happy memory) of St. Augustine, "I wasn't there and didn't see it." But the scene of the pretty story is alleged at Tampa.

In this delightful, balmy air some days that are like spring days may be whiled away and most pleasantly, or a whole season, if it were not that we are *en route* for Havana and must hence to

PORT TAMPA,

where embark. To avoid lighterage and a transfer of passengers from the cars to the ship, the railway was extended down the bay to opposite deep water, and a long pier built out to the channel and tracks laid so that trains could run alongside the ship.

On the pier over the water, at high or low tide, always over the water, is built an inn. A unique little house with excellent accommodations for thirty or forty people, where tourists may wait and rest, or wait for trains or ships, if ever need be. The Inn on the Pier at Port Tampa must become a resort for fishers and hunters up and down the coast, and as they stop at the Inn, need not lose any time, but fish from the galleries or a bedroom window. The Inn is new, but it has its fish story, a tarpon story. A tarpon over six feet long has been taken by hook and line held on the pier. While the Inn was intended for accommodation of through passengers between this country and Cuba, it is not confined to their uses. It is a resort for tourists also, and this Inn being on the pier, is the peer of any Inn in the country.

Now the anchor is weighed, all sail is set, and the good ship is headed for Key West.

The ships "Mascotte" and "Olivette" leave Port Tampa on the arrival of the West India Fast Mail with the through sleeper from New York, which is at night. The electric search-light shows the dim outline of the shore, the islands and keys down the bay, and the buoys which mark the way. The first hours of the voyage are as plain and easy sailing as on a lake, though the first look from a state-room window in the morning shows only water, water everywhere—and land nowhere to be seen. Sometimes, when the day is very clear, looking from the port side a distant palm may be seen far to the eastward, on an island, or perhaps the coast of Florida; and shortly after noon a sharp lookout ahead and a little to the port side will show some more palm trees, at first only little specks between sky and water; these are on the Florida Keys, and very soon Key West is designated. The palms grow taller, and then the shore line comes to view, and every moment is of interest till the lines are made fast to the pier at Key West.

The steamers of the Plant Line always call at Key West, both on the going and returning voyage, for freights and mails. Ask the purser or captain for how long they stop—often there is time for a ramble or a drive around the Island. Key West is not an extensive domain, but what it lacks in acreage it makes up in tropic beauty. Here is found what is earnestly hunted for in all other Florida—palm trees, not palmettos—genuine "feathery palms," of which the poets write, and underneath them all, the plants and flowers that grow in the tropics. Some pretty cottages are almost hidden in the dense foliage, and are only discovered by the white paint with which they are all adorned. This is the most southerly of all of Uncle Sam's possessions and the most interesting, and that same sense of security which pervades a back county in Indiana is not lost on this little island in the sea—though I don't think this is the result of a knowledge of the presence of Fort Taylor—a huge brick house with portholes instead of windows, garrisoned (when I was there) by a corporal's guard, a lot of rusty cannon and some cows. The tourist is not impressed with a formidableness of our coast defenses by a visit to Fort Taylor.

When the ship comes in there are a lot of carriages at the dock, just as if it was an

American railway train arriving at an inland station. I don't mean a Fifth avenue carriage—these are rockaways, barouches and carry-alls, which have seen better days, drawn by horses that some day in the near future may do a grand *finale* in the *plaza de toros*, at Havana. The distance of a drive around the island is not great, and even with the vehicles at hand, the chances of a return to the ship in due time is in the tourist's favor. I remember one barouche drawn by a white horse, which in turn was driven by a red-headed boy. When I say driven, I mean it, because the horse didn't seem to enter into the zest of the drive at all, but he was persuaded by vigorous prods at the hand of the boy. I chose this turnout, not for its glittering get up,—really I don't know why I did choose this one because they all look alike—now that it is all over, and I come to think of it, perhaps there was luck in the combination of the white horse and the red-headed boy, anyhow I was back at the pier on time and enjoyed the drive very much.

When the ship leaves Key West it leaves the United States, and though the distance across the Gulf Stream is short, is just as much at sea as if in the middle of the Atlantic, and the sensation as novel and pleasant—or otherwise—either way it is not for long. The departure is not hurried nor is the ship pushed to full headway, as no entrance to the harbor of Havana is made till sunrise, and there is no hurry. After watching the lights on the keys and the stars that are brighter in these skies than any other, there is nothing left for the night but the seclusion a state-room grants.

If by chance your window opens on the port side when the next sun shines, its rays will come to you over the watch towers and walls of Morro Castle and Cabaña ; if on the starboard side, it will light up the domes and crosses of the churches in Havana. The soldiers in the Castle have just answered another reveille, and may be the relief guards are just on the parapets with glistening guns and swords ; and if you watch the flag staff—see the Plant colors run up, as if to salute the favorite ship of the Cubans, and announcing the arrival safe in port of returning friends, or the welcome of tourists to *La Isla de Cuba*. On the other side the ship the city is just awakening—Havana don't get up early. The ship steams slowly up the little harbor, drops her anchor, and we are in Cuba. The other pages tell what to do now.

After Cuba, then what ?

The tour of the Island only whets the desire for further voyages in these summer seas—from Havana. ships sail to all parts of the world, and particularly to the others of the West India Islands. Tickets for these voyages and full information may be obtained at the offices of the Plant Line, in New York, Jacksonville or Havana.

A TOUR OF THE WEST INDIES.

The Royal Mail Steam Packet Co., under contract with Her Majesty of England for the conveyance of the mails, sails from Havana to Jamaica, thence to England. From Jamaica the tourist may sail from island to island on ships going on regular dates. thus taking up the winter in short sea-voyages and tours of the loveliest islands in all the seas ; return can be made to Havana at any time.

ANTIGUA

is the most important of the Leeward Islands and the residence of the Governor-in-Chief. It differs in configuration from all the other Leeward Islands, having no central ridge of mountains ; the main elevation follows the coast line, which is also varied by numerous beautiful bays. Specimens of various kinds of fossils and petrified wood are very plentiful ; there are also many species of land shells to be found. A delicacy belonging to the Island is the Mangrove Oyster. About forty miles to the southwest lies Montserrat, presenting on a small scale all the varied beauties of tropical scenery, being very mountainous, well wooded, and with numerous springs ; it is the headquarters of Lime cultivation.

BARBADOS

is the most windward of the Caribbee Islands, is most densely populated, and is the most thriving of the British West India Islands.   The Island is about the size and height of the Isle of Wight, and from being cultivated throughout, and comparatively level, it affords more opportunities of exercise than many others.   The roads are excellent, and many pretty drives can be taken through the Island.   A few miles from Bridge-town, the capital, is a watering place, called Hastings, where good sea-bathing can be obtained.   The highest land is in the northeastern quarter, which is hilly and bleak ; its greatest elevation is about 1,100 feet above the sea.   Bridgetown has a Cathedral and some handsome houses.

DEMERARA.

George Town, the capital of British Guiana, is a handsome city, containing many fine buildings.   The principal streets are perfectly straight, with good carriage roads. The hotel accommodation is good, and there are, besides, two club-houses.   The scenery in the interior, and up the Essequibo river, is most beautiful and romantic.

DOMINICA

is a large island, having an area of 275 square miles ; it presents magnificent scenery, and only requires capital and labor to become a flourishing colony.   Its central por-tions are covered with high mountains.   A boiling lake, hitherto entirely unknown, was recently discovered by an English visitor.   The principal town is Roseau, on the southwest coast.

GRENADA

is said to be the most beautiful of the Caribbees ; it abounds in streams and mineral and other springs.   The mountains that occupy the interior rise to 3,200 feet above the sea.   In the northwest are successive piles of conical hills or continuous ridges, covered with vast forest trees and brushwood.   Its mountains form many fertile valleys, interspersed with numerous rivulets.

GUADALOUPE

is one of the most valuable West India Colonies belonging to France.   It consists properly of two islands, separated from each other by a narrow channel.   The western division of the island, called Basse Terre, is the most important, and is divided into two parts by a ridge of very rugged mountains, extending north and south.   Toward the south point there appears a mountain, called La Souffriére, or Sulphur Hill, which is about 5,500 feet above the level of the sea.   This mountain exhales a thick black smoke, mixed with sparks.   The chief town of Guadaloupe is named Basse Terre, situated near the south end of the island.

JAMAICA

is the largest and most valuable of the West India Islands belonging to Great Britain, was discovered by Columbus in 1494.   From the sea level on all sides of Jamaica a series of ridges gradually ascend toward the central ranges from which they radiate, dividing the great rivers, and attaining in the culminating western peak of the Blue Mountains an elevation of 7,335 feet.   From these mountains at least seventy streams descend to the north and south shores, but, with the exception of one (the Black River), they are not navigable.   The mountains are covered with many kinds of trees, and in the valleys are such a variety of fruit trees as to give the country a most fertile and pleasing appearance. The scenery of this magnificent island is truly delightful. The predominant features of the landscape are grandeur and sublimity. There are two railroads now, one on the south side to the village of Poms and then by stage to Mandeville, in the Manchester Mountains ; the other through the Bog-walk, so well known for its scenery, to the foot of St. Ann's Mountains, thence to the north side of St. Ann's Bay, or Ocho River's magnificent scenery. The roads throughout the island are excellent.

Jamaica may be reckoned among the most romantic and highly diversified countries in the world ; uniting rich magnificent scenery with waving forests, never-failing streams, and constant verdure, heightened by a pure atmosphere and the glowing tints of a tropical sun.

The rivers, including springs and rivulets, have been estimated at upward of 200 in number. From the mountainous nature of the country, and the huge masses of rock that frequently obstruct their course, they are often precipitous, and exhibit numerous and beautiful cascades, bursting headlong in the foam and thunder of a cataract. The population of Kingston, the capital, is estimated at 40,000.

MARTINIQUE

belongs to France, and is the largest island in the West Indies belonging to that country ; its scenery is exceedingly beautiful. The two principal cities are Saint Pierre and Fort-de-France, where very good hotel accommodation can be obtained ; at the former place there is a handsome opera-house, and botanical gardens about a mile from the town. The Empress Josephine, and her first husband, Viscount Beauharnais, were natives of this island.

PORT-AU-PRINCE,

the capital of the Republic of Hayti, contains about 21,000 inhabitants. The Republic of Hayti is the western portion of the Island of St. Domingo. The Republic of San Domingo is confined to the eastern portion of the island, which is, next to Cuba, the largest of the West India Islands. The mountains are richly and heavily timbered, and susceptible of cultivation nearly to their summits. It is probably the most fertile spot in the West Indies, whilst its excellent harbors offer considerable facilities to foreign trade. The principal productions are mahogany, logwood, coffee, cotton, tobacco and sugar.

ST. KITTS

is the oldest of the British colonies in the West Indies. Mount Misery, the highest peak of the central ridge of mountains, 4,000 feet above the sea level, is of tolerably easy ascent ; it is a mass of rock projecting from the lip of a large crater, the descent into which is a work of some toil, but well worth making. Volcanic action is by no means extinct, there being a short distance up one side of the crater hundreds of sulphurous jets too hot for the hand to be held over them. After heavy rains the bottom of the crater becomes a lake of several acres in extent, with a mean depth of five or six feet. Across the main ridge there is a pathway practicable for mules or ponies, which served for communication between the English settlements on the opposite side of the island at the time when it was partly in French occupation. Brimstone Hill, standing close to the shore, and looking as though pitched there out of the crater whose bowl it would about fill up, has upon it the remains of magnificent fortifications, no longer applied to any use ; before the days of rifled artillery the fortress was looked upon as impregnable—the Gibraltar of the West Indies.

In the island may be found some two hundred species of well-marked varieties of ferns. Near St. Kitts is the Island of Nevis, where the warm baths supplied from some sulphur springs are held in high repute for rheumatic affections, and are resorted to from very remote parts.

TRINIDAD,

the most southerly, and, next to Jamaica, the largest of the British West India Islands. The chief town, Port of Spain, is one of the finest towns in the West Indies, and contains about 25,000 inhabitants. The "Pitch Lake" in the southwest corner of the island is a wonderful phenomenon ; it covers about 150 acres. Not only are the mountains of this magnificent island beautifully wooded, but there are several rivers navigable far into the interior, irrigating and affording communication with thousands of acres of land. The waterfalls and blue basin, both within a few miles of Port of Spain, are well worth a visit, and the hot springs and mud volcanoes should also be seen.

The average American is in a hurry, but when he is interested, he will not go home as long as any other place is open, and while the longest way round is not always the nearest home, it is often the most interesting, and with this idea in view, it is suggested to take a sail to Vera Cruz, and return to the United States

THROUGH MEXICO.

Steamers leave Havana at frequent intervals regularly, sometimes two or three times a week ; some of them touching at Campeché, Progreso, and other Yucatan ports, but all going to Vera Cruz.

The Mexican Railway from Vera Cruz to the City of Mexico passes some of the finest scenery in the world, and from the City of Mexico there are three lines of railway to the United States, running direct, of excellent equipment, including Pullman cars to the border at Laredo, Eagle Pass, and El Paso, connecting at those places with other lines with through Pullmans for St. Louis and New Orleans, making the possibilities for comforts of such a tour all that could be desired.

IN THE CITY OF MEXICO.

Some centuries ago, when Cortez came to the crest of the eastern hills, looked over the plain of Mexico and saw the fair city sitting like a jewel in the midst of it, he must have felt that *there* was his reward for weary marches and hard-fought battles.

When the traveler of to-day looks from the windows of a palace car as it rolls over the crest of the Sierra Madres, or through the Tajo de Nochistongo at Huehuetoca, and sees the plain, the same old city and lake with the everlasting hills around about, circling it as with a girdle—sees the white-capped giants Ixtacciwhatl and Popocatapetl doing eternal vigil, a never-ending sentinel duty over all, he must feel that the journey from wherever it may be, was worth all the traveling. Mexico is more of a metropolitan city than is generally supposed or its appearance indicates, and the means of getting about, comfortable and convenient, and reasonable withal. At the railway station will be found all kinds of hacks, ready to do your bidding at all kinds of prices. They carry little tin flags which indicate the class of vehicle and the tariff. Those with a green flag make a rate of $1.50 per hour or 75 cents per single passenger for a short drive within a district ; the blue flag hires for $1 by the hour or 50 cents per passenger ; the red, 75 cents per hour or 25 cents per passenger : the white flags are the cheapest, being only 50 cents per hour or whatever the passenger will pay, and if the red or white flags are selected, it is purely from an economical point of view, with no pretense to style of rig, and with no particular desire as to when the destination is to be reached. If overcharges are made, and Mexican hackmen are not unlike their American brethren, ask for the number— *Numero* is the word to use, and he will usually lapse to tariff rates. If a carriage is wanted for a single trip, simply call the name of the place ; if by the hour say " *Por hora*," and the prices will be given as above ; green flags, " *un peso y cuatro reales ;* " blue, *un peso ;* red, *seis reales ;* white, *cuatro reales.*

HORSE CARS.

The street-car system in the City of Mexico is a good one, reaching all railway stations and nearly every point of interest in and around the city. Fares in the city *un medio* (6¼ cents), to the suburbs *un real* (12½), and *dos reales* (25 cents), according to the distance traveled. These are first-class fares, the tariff in second-class cars being much cheaper, but are only patronized by the poorer classes. The second-class cars are painted green and follow a half block behind the yellow first-class cars.

The driver carries a tin horn, not unlike the campaign horn of the United States, and which he blows as assiduously, as a note of warning at street intersections. Conductors sell tickets and a collector gets on the cars at certain points of the route and takes them up. The street-car companies do not confine their operations to the passenger business solely, they do a freight business as well. Another feature of their business approaches the trade of the undertaker. Each line has its funeral car, black, with a four-poster pagoda surmounted by a cross, under which is a black catafalque. An arrangement of this

SPANISH LADY.

kind is cheaper than the hearse and carriages. You order a funeral car to be at the nearest point to the residence, the corpse is put on board and the mourners follow in the other cars, regular or special, and instead of paying for carriages you simply pay so much per mourner. But this is a digression from the tourist topic. Carriages are necessary for a proper seeing of the Paseo and to save a long walk up a steep hill at the end of the tracks at Chapultepec.

THE PASEO,

or, to be explicit, the Paseo de la Reforma, is *the* drive of the city. It is about two and a half miles long, reaches from the city to Chapultepec, and is a magnificent boulevard, where the *bon ton* are pleased to drive every afternoon from four o'clock till dark, when the magnificent procession of fine equipages files down San Francisco street and disperses.

was once the favorite park of Moctezuma ; later the palace built there by one of the Viceroys of Spain (Galvey) was used by Maximilian, and is now the residence of the President, the Mexican White House. The park and hill was the scene of a conflict between the United States troops and Mexicans in 1847, when the hill was carried by assault. Besides the presidential residence, the National Military Academy is also located here. A pass to the buildings may be had from the Governor of the National Palace in the city.

GUADALOUPE.

Horse-cars run from the Plaza Mayor, the Cathedral, to Guadaloupe half hourly, along the ancient causeway. Along the way are numerous shrines where religious processions were wont to stop for devotional purposes, but the cars proceed on their way to the village about a league from the city, and stop in front of the church at the foot of the hill where the shrine of Guadaloupe is. Passing through a little garden or park to the right of the church, one comes to a small chapel in the entrance of which is a fountain of pure, clear water, which is said to have gushed forth on the spot where the Virgin stood when she appeared to Juan Diego. From this spot around the corner of a narrow street, are some stone stairs leading to the shrine or chapel on the crest of the hill where Juan gathered the flowers, and is one of the most picturesque spots in all Mexico. On ascending the stairs, may be seen on the right near the top, what seems to be a ship's mast with sails all set, done in stone. A legend says that some storm-tossed sailors prayed to the Virgin of Guadaloupe and vowed that if they were saved from a watery grave they would carry the mast to the shrine and erect it there as a memorial and thank-offering—which 'tis said they did carry it from Vera Cruz, incased it in stone, and erected it where it stands to-day.

On the line to Tacuba, which was once a causeway, is the place of "*el salto de Alvarado*" (the leap of Alvarado), where that warrior made his famous leap for life. The exact spot, as shown, is in front of the *Tivoli del Elisco*. At the end of the causeway, near the church of St. Esteban, is the tree of *Noche Triste* (the dismal night), where Cortez sat down and cried after his defeat. The tree is a giant *ahuehuete* or cypress, of great age, now enclosed with an iron rail to prevent a recurrence of further vandalism, as occurred some years ago, by a crank having set it on fire. There are cranks in Mexico, too.

The floating gardens, *Chinampas*, on the Viga canal, are reached by horse-cars from the Plaza Mayor, near the Cathedral, to Embarcadero, and thence by canoe for a few hours or for a day.

THE CATHEDRAL AND THE CHURCHES.

It is not expected to describe them here, there are one hundred and twenty-seven of them, and it is a never-ending tale of towers, bells, crosses, images, pictures and legends from beginning to end, from San Domingo, of Inquisition fame, and San Hipolito, mentioned with the slaughter of the *noche triste*, to the Cathedral, which is a grand aggregation of all styles and designs of church architecture in Mexico, so that any detail of the story cannot be expected here.

The Mint, the National Palace, the National Museum, are all places of interest, in the centre of the city, which can be visited in the walks about town. The Museum is rich in antiquities of bygone ages, and the relics of fallen and past dynasties in the country's history, which must be older than Egypt, reading from examples of Aztec picture writing, Moctezuma's shield and the statue of *Huitzilopochtli*, the god of war, down to Maximilian's coach of state and his dinner service.

In the National Library are over 200,000 volumes, in all languages. Old books and new; books over 400 years old; books on vellum and parchment; books that the British Museum has not got, but would like to have. There is an atlas of England, printed in Amsterdam in 1659, with steel plates and in colors that are as bright and fresh as if just off the press. Another volume bears date of 1472, and another is still older, printed in two colors, with a most perfect register. There is a Spanish and Mexican dictionary, printed in Mexico in 1571. There is a book of autographs of notables and soldiers of Cortez. A roll of deerskin shows some original dispatches (painted pictures) sent by Moctezuma to his allies, but intercepted by Cortez. There are original manuscripts and immense volumes with every old English letter done with a pen. There are rare books of all ages and nations, from a Chinese dictionary to Picturesque B. & O., and a copy of the POINTER.

The *Monte Piedad* is the national "uncle" of the impecunious Mexican; here he brings his pledges and borrows what they will bring. The institution was established to lend money on collateral at a low rate of interest, and is under direct control of the Government. Unredeemed pledges are exposed for sale at a certain price; if not sold within a given time they are marked lower, and after a while still lower, and thus often some rare bargains in old jewels and heirlooms are obtained.

The theatres are the *Principal, Arbeu, National, Alarcon* and *Hidalgo*, which, with Orrin's Circus forms amusement for the city, excepting always the bull fights. The non-Spanish-speaking American will hardly be amused at the theatres, but at the circus cannot fail to be pleased.

The *Alameda* and the *Zocalo* are the places of resort by the people at all times, where they come for rest and recreation, come to walk under the shade of the trees. or sit among the flowers, and listen to the melodies of their country, listen to music that is the gift of the Government to its people. On Sundays and feast days, and in the evenings during the week, military bands play at this park or the other, so there is music somewhere all the time.

The markets are interesting to every tourist; all the fruits of the tropics are there, fresh from the gardens and groves of the "hot lands," only a few leagues away. All the vegetables of this country, and which are grown in summer here, are in the stalls there in January.

And as to flowers—I have seen great bunches of violets in the glass-covered pagoda under the shadow of the Cathedral, go begging sale at a *tlaco;* a handful of roses, worth a dollar each in New York, offered for a *medio;* a basket of flowers for a *real,* and one two feet high for a half-dollar ; I saw all this the day I read of the fearful blizzard at home, and wondered at such a climate that could produce them in a country nearly 8,000 feet above the sea.

The markets of Merced and Volador are just a square or two south of the Palace, and a little farther on is the canal, with its waters covered with boats and the banks with the hucksters. The San Juan and Catarina are on the squares of the same name, all with more or less interest to the visitor.

And last of all where you will go to are the cemeteries; San Fernando contains the tombs of some of the Presidents, and its great soldiers, and is also the resting place of Miramon and Mejio, who were executed with Maximilian. Another cemetery near Tacubaya is the Dolores, where there are some fine monuments. The Americans, English and Spanish have separate burial places.

I have written of the horse-car funeral trains. I have seen other queer funeral parties, and sadder ones. I have seen a man and woman get into a second-class car, he with a tiny coffin in his arms, and I have seen two Indians walking solemnly along the street with a longer coffin on their shoulders, while the mourners, too poor for even a horse-car fare, followed on foot. These are the exception, the brighter scenes in Mexico are many, and one never tires of a visit to the ancient city of the Moctezumas.

The Mexican National Railway runs from the City of Mexico to Laredo ; the stopping places of interest to the tourist are Toluca, Celaya, San Miguel de Allende, San Luis Potosi, Saltillo, Monterey and Topo Chico Hot Springs. The Mexican Central to El Paso ; Querétaro, Celaya, Silao, Leon, Aguas Calientes, Zacatecas, Lerdo and Chihuahua are all fine cities of many attractions. The Mexican International to Eagle Pass, passing those cities of the Mexican Central as far north as Torreon ; then on the main line of the International are Parras, Sabinas and Monclova, where stop-over tickets may be asked for. These lines are all under American managements and offer every facility found on railways in the United States. The management of the Plant lines will effect the sale of a ticket covering a tour of Florida, Cuba, the West Indies, Mexico and return to starting point in the United States. I have seen it advertised for summer travelers to take a ride of a thousand miles through the Colorado mountains, and return again to the point of starting and the tour was denominated

AROUND THE CIRCLE.

What an "around the circle " this is for a winter tour ; through Florida to Tampa, thence to Key West and Havana, to Vera Cruz, circling the Gulf of Mexico, and returning home through Mexico ; not *one* thousand miles, but three or four, not over mountains, but over summer seas in winter days.

www.ingramcontent.com/pod-product-compliance
Lightning Source LLC
Chambersburg PA
CBHW031819090426
42739CB00008B/1339